Into the
World Next Door

Stories of hope and adventure from
an unlikely journey around the world

Bob & Pat,
Thank you for helping make
WND a reality! It's been
great to be your neighbor. :)
Barry Rodriguez

by Barry Rodriguez

Be strong and courageous. Do not be terrified; do not be discouraged, for the Lord your God will be with you wherever you go.

Joshua 1:9

CONTENTS

Introduction

It is absurd you're reading this book right now. Patently ridiculous.

Don't get me wrong. There's nothing wrong with *you*. I just mean the fact this book exists at *all* is completely nuts. The idea that I (*Me! Barry!*) would have experienced all the things in the pages you're about to read… well, it's crazy.

Here's why. A decade ago I was a comfort-loving, picky-eating video game addict. I was lazy, I was unmotivated, and I didn't have an adventurous bone in my body. My faith consisted of going to church on the weekends, reading a few Christian-ey books every now and then, and trying not to sin too much. Sure, I had attended three years of Bible school, but going into full-time ministry was looking less and less likely every day.

I was not - *in any way* - a globe-trotting Indiana Jones type with jet black hair and a rippling six pack. I was not - *in any way* - cut out for life in slums or refugee camps or mountain villages. I had no foundation of trust in God with which to jump boldly into the unknown. I had no awareness of my own self-centered worldview. What I *did* have was asthma, acne, and allergies. I had a weak stomach, poor endurance, and a penchant for whining loudly when I felt uncomfortable.

So you get the picture, right? It makes no sense that you're reading this book right now.

And yet.

I say those words a lot these days. And yet.

And yet God chose me, *of all people,* to go on this whirlwind journey. God chose me, *of all people,* to eat fried tarantula in Cambodia, to fight off rats on a bed in South Sudan, to vomit from dehydration on a Panamanian mountainside, and to sleep homeless in a New York train station.

God chose me, *of all people*, to see the ongoing effects of apartheid in South Africa, to hear tales of injustice on a Native American reservation, to talk with genocide survivors in Rwanda, and to observe the ongoing hostilities between Israel and Palestine.

And God chose me, *of all people*, to witness the mind-bending compassion of Christ-followers in a Ukrainian orphanage, to learn at the feet of an Indian social reformer, to live with a pastor's family in a Kenyan slum, and to discover the soul transformation happening among trafficked girls in Cambodia.

Needless to say, it is unbelievably humbling to have had all these experiences. It is a great privilege to have had so much exposure to the world. The amount I have changed, grown, and developed through this season can hardly be overstated.

Which is why I wrote this book. I don't want to take this life-change for granted. I don't want to keep it all for myself. I am desperate for the transformation of my life to be a catalyst for the transformation of yours. Because let's be real here. If God could use *me* to accomplish some of his kingdom[1] purposes, imagine how he could use *you*!

---

[1] I reference the kingdom of God a LOT in this book. The kingdom, described by Jesus many times in the Bible, is simply a reference to the rule and reign of God in this world - his mission of redemption, hope, love, healing, and justice being accomplished.

—

OK. So let me tell you a little bit about this crazy, ridiculous, unlikely book.

The chapters that follow are mostly stories I experienced while running the ministry I started in 2009. It was called World Next Door. The ministry was my attempt to use stories, photos, and compelling next-steps to help *other* suburban Christ-followers like me get more engaged with God's kingdom, especially as it pertained to the poor and marginalized in the world.

To my great surprise, the ministry was quite a success. Because of our stories we saw orphans adopted, children sponsored, providential building campaigns completed, families relocated to serve internationally, many decisions made to go on short term trips, lots of new financial commitments to our partner organizations, the lives of 19 summer interns and 6 year-long journalism fellows changed forever, and much more. It was quite a ride. The story of how I ended up actually *starting* the ministry is in one of the chapters of the book, so I won't get into that here.

All you need to know is that the last six years of my life have been spent traveling all over the world, embedding with indigenous, Christ-centered organizations, sitting at the feet of these ministries' leaders, and learning everything I could along the way. As I traveled, I wrote many, many blog posts and articles about my experiences - far too many to capture in one book. As a result, there are quite a few stories and overarching narratives that didn't make the cut.

The fact is, the last six years have been a wild hodgepodge of growth, learning, and experiences. I've learned a million things from a million people in a million different ways. Trying to cram all that into a neat, tidy package just wasn't going to happen. So I didn't even try. Instead, I wrote *this* book. It's not a perfectly organized summary of my experiences. It's not a comprehensive guide to the things I've learned. It's not even in chronological order. These chapters are simply, for lack of a better term, my heart's "greatest hits." They're the stories I tell over and over to anyone who will listen because they have *blown my mind*. They're the memories of hope I cling to when things are looking grim. They're the life lessons I don't ever want to forget.

Some of the stories are quite short. Others are a bit longer. Each can stand alone, but you'll see many common themes emerge when they're taken together. My guess is that once you've read this book, you'll understand why I consider the last six years to be the most ridiculously eye-opening, heart-breaking, life-changing season of my life. My hope, of course, is that you, too, will be changed by these stories. I hope as you read these accounts your own heart is stirred and your imagination is ignited. I hope you are inspired by this glimpse into God's global kingdom at work.

—

Like I said at the beginning, the book you're holding right now is absurd. It's ridiculous. But it's here, and I couldn't be more thrilled. So turn the page, friend! When you do, you'll be reading a book that only exists because our God is strong where we are weak, loves to do the impossible, and obviously has a sense of humor.

1

Romaniv

Extreme Makeover: Україна Edition.

This is how it ends, I thought. *I'm going to die.*

Knuckles clenched around the edge of my seat, I saw my death approaching. Birch trees whizzed by as our van careened down the road. We roared past puttering trucks and ancient Soviet-era cars. Occasionally, we whipped around a blind curve in the passing lane, swerving back onto our side of the road just moments before slamming into oncoming traffic. Each time, I held my breath, gripped the seat a bit tighter, and wondered why Ukrainians never seemed to wear seat belts.

I tried to take my cues from the rest of the people in our van. My traveling companions were Mission to Ukraine staff and volunteers who had been down this road countless times before. They chatted amiably, seemingly unaware of the giant metallic objects hurtling past us at near the speed of sound. They didn't seem fazed by the danger of our situation, so I took a few deep breaths and tried to listen in to their conversation.

Oksana Shulyak and Yulya Bochkovska were talking about Romaniv Disabled Boys Orphanage, our destination on this clear morning in April of 2009. From what I understood, Mission to Ukraine (MTU) had been visiting the orphanage every week for a year as part of their mission to love and serve people with special needs. I would be going with them during one of these weekly visits.

The existence of an orphanage dedicated *just* to disabled boys struck me as rather strange. It seemed oddly specific. But I quickly learned that Romaniv Orphanage was just one of *many* such institutions in Ukraine. Because of rampant poverty, deep cultural stigmas left over from the Soviet era, and a huge lack of education about disabilities, life in Ukraine was rough for families of children with special needs. Other than a small financial stipend, these families got virtually no support from the government or their communities. There weren't even wheelchair ramps in Zhytomyr, the city where MTU was located.

Many parents of kids with special needs chose to hand them over to the care of the state, rather than struggle to raise them alone. As a result, each Ukrainian "oblast" (state) had its own network of orphanages for children with disabilities. Romaniv was one of them.

As we got closer to the orphanage, I began to breathe a bit easier. The dirt road made suicidal speeds impossible. I knew we'd live a bit longer (until our return journey, at least). My discomfort shifted into something new, however, when Oksana turned to give me a few guidelines about our visit. At one point she said, "It's hard. Going to Romaniv is sometimes very difficult for people, so it's OK if you want to step outside during the class."

This made me nervous. At that point in my life, I *had* begun to travel and do more out-of-the-box things, but I had *not* spent very much time working with disabilities. I didn't know how to act. I didn't know what to do. I was perfectly fine offering a kind smile when I met someone with special needs, but going to an orphanage *full* of boys with disabilities was intimidating, to say the least. I didn't know how I'd respond to what we were about to see.

———

Lost in thought, I was surprised when the van came to a stop. We had arrived at a nondescript archway on the side of a tree lined avenue. It was the entrance to Romaniv Disabled Boys Orphanage. The team piled out of the van, gathered supplies for class, and started walking through the main gates of the orphanage. I looked around, eyes wide, at what can only be described as institutional desolation. Crumbling buildings stood in a row along a red brick pathway. On the other side of the path were about 20-30 trees with their tops chopped off. It must have once been an orchard of some kind, but these trees looked more like skeletons than anything else. Despite the blue sky, billowy clouds, and sunshine, I felt a profound sense of gloominess as we walked up to the main building to see the boys.

For some reason, I was the first of our group to enter. My heart pounded as I opened the outside door. Immediately I was overwhelmed by a putrid stench. It was like sticking my face into an open sewer. I fought back the urge to gag and retch as we walked further into the building.

That's when I heard the boys. Like someone turning up the dial on a stereo, I was assaulted by a cacophony of unfamiliar and unsettling sounds. One boy was screaming. Another was singing loudly. Several young men were humming to themselves while others banged their fists against the wall. I couldn't make sense of any of it.

Time had slowed to a crawl. All of these smells and sounds hit my overwhelmed brain in the time it took to walk the ten feet from the outer to inner doors. When we finally opened the inside doors, I could barely think straight. I didn't have a context for any of this. It was sensory overload.

Then I saw the boys and simply froze in my tracks. At least 60 boys and young men with a whole range of physical and mental disabilities were crammed into two tiny rooms. Many were sitting on benches lining the bare walls, some were wandering aimlessly in the middle of the room, and a few were huddled in the corner of an open coat closet. I watched in horror as one boy repeatedly banged his head against the wall. Another kept punching himself in the chin. One boy was standing in a puddle of his own urine.

I didn't know what to do. A few of the boys walked up to me with huge smiles and shouts of "Privyet!" ("Hello!"), extending their hands for me to shake. Many of them had cuts and sores on their faces. A few had mouths full of brown, rotting teeth. To my shame, I felt an urge to back away. The moment was a nightmare for my germaphobic sensibility. Somehow I managed to shake a few of the boys' hands, trying desperately to paste a sincere-looking smile on my face. Yet again, I wondered what in the world I had gotten myself into.

Just then, the rest of the MTU team entered the building. With huge smiles and energetic greetings, they rushed around me like a river, sweeping the boys up into big bear hugs, touching their faces, tousling their hair, and putting their arms around the young men's shoulders. They seemed to know the names of almost every boy, and the boys knew them right back.

"Oksana! Oksana!" the boys called out, eager to show Oksana Shulyak the beaded bracelets they had made the week before. Without fail, Oksana smiled and said, "Wow. Molodets!" ("Well done!")

Within moments, MTU staff and volunteers were setting up materials for the day's lesson, hooking up the stereo for music, and trying to get the boys to sit quietly. I retreated behind my camera for a moment, catching my breath and trying to compose myself while snapping a few photos. I had trouble grasping what I was seeing. The squalor of the boys' condition was one thing. Seeing the carefree love and affection by my new Ukrainian friends was something else entirely. How were they able to act so *normal* around these young men?

The class officially started when Oksana Kolomiichuk[2] rang

---

[2] Oksana is a very common name in Ukraine, so I'll refer to them

a small hand bell. She passed it around the circle, smiling and offering encouragements as each boy rang the bell in turn. One of the boys had trouble shaking the bell, so Oksana S gently put her hands around his, then helped him ring it. The smile of pride on his face after this small accomplishment hit me like a ton of bricks. So much joy from something so simple!

Romaniv boys in a coat closet during my first visit

Once Oksana K began her lesson for the day, teaching about the different seasons, I noticed an empty spot on the bench between two of the boys. At this point, I was so far out of my comfort zone I had lost all reason to hold back anymore. I took a seat. One of the boys grabbed my hand and shook it. His fingers were wet. I wasn't sure with what. I put my arms around his shoulder and held on tight, fighting back tears at the complexity of this moment.

—

Mission to Ukraine first visited Romaniv Orphanage a year before my visit. Their ministry had long focused on teaching, loving, and caring for children with special needs in Zhytomyr, but they had felt compelled to expand their reach to love on

as "Oksana S" and "Oksana K" from this point forward.

disabled kids *without* any parents. When they first toured the orphanage, they were shocked at its deplorable conditions. The walls were painted black. There were bars on the windows. Some of the boys were chained to their beds. Nestled away on the edge of a town in the middle of nowhere, Romaniv was like a landfill for unwanted human refuse. Thanks in large part to the perspective of Ukraine's post-soviet culture, the boys' disabilities were seen as shameful, embarrassing, and often too much for their biological families to deal with.

After touring the facility for the first time, the MTU team met with the orphanage administration and explained that they wanted to teach the boys. They wanted to make the one hour drive from Zhytomyr every single week to lead classes, sing songs, and educate the young men at Romaniv.

The administrators were incredulous. "Why would you want to do that? These boys are just like animals. You can *try* to teach them but it won't do anything. You'll give up in a month."

Despite the doubts, MTU stayed true to its commitment to send a team every week. By the time of my visit, one year later, they had made a bit of progress. The walls had been re-painted. The bars had been taken off the windows. But the administration was still very skeptical about the value of these weekly classes. *Nobody* paid attention to these boys. *Nobody* tried to change their situation. With all their disabilities, they thought, what was the point?

—

As I sat in the class that day, watching the MTU team living out the kingdom of God so practically, my mind was running on overdrive. On the outside, I was smiling and laughing and singing with the boys. On the inside, I was a swirl of emotion. I was horrified to see the conditions in which these young men lived. I was elated to see how tenderly they were loved by Mission to Ukraine. I was ashamed at my initial revulsion. Witnessing the limits of my own compassion was a majorly humbling experience. It was an emotional roller coaster.

Towards the end of class, Yulya brought in a pitcher, a bar

of soap, a towel, and a small blue basin filled with water. The other volunteers gathered the boys and did their best to help them form a line. Then, one by one, the boys were taught how to wash their own hands. It took me a second to register this. *They had never been taught how to wash their own hands.*

Some of the boys thought it was a game. One of them tried to lick the soap. But despite their confusion, the volunteers patiently walked each of the boys through the process, offering words of guidance, encouragement, and affirmation along the way.

"Yes! Take the soap. Now move your hands back and forth. Good job!"

"No, don't put your hands down there. That's the dirty water."

"OK, take the towel and dry your hands. Well done!"

Before I knew it, the activity was over, class had ended, and we were saying goodbye to the boys. There were hugs all around, a few high fives, and many shouts of "Paka paka!" ("See you later!"). Moments later, we were walking out of the classroom building, standing on the brick pathway, and breathing fresh air once more.

It was like emerging from a dream. I didn't know what to feel. I didn't know what to think. One of the volunteers asked me, "So, how was it?" All I could say was, "Um. Wow." Relieved to be done for the day, I eagerly looked forward to heading back to Zhytomyr for some much-needed processing time.

Yulya was the last of our team to leave the building. She walked down the steps, turned to me and said, "Now comes the really hard part."

I didn't know what she was referring to. I thought we were done. As it turned out, we had yet to visit the so-called "isolation building," the section of the orphanage for the *severely* disabled boys.

I took a deep breath and wondered how anything could be worse than what we had just seen.

We made our way down the path to the isolation building,

walked up the steps (there were no wheelchair ramps at Romaniv), and entered yet another building that smelled worse than a barn. Inside were another 30 boys, most of whom faced far greater disabilities than the ones we had met before. Several of them were in wheelchairs, a few had startling physical deformities, and a number of them had severe forms of autism. All of them - all 30 boys - were being watched by just two orphanage caretakers.

Yet again, we set up crafts, sang a few songs, and led some of the higher functioning boys through a class. I watched, wide-eyed, as the MTU team did their best to interact with each of the attention-starved boys. There were tickles, smiles, and conversations. One team member simply wrapped her arms around a boy in her lap and held him tightly the whole time. He had a look of sheer bliss on his face.

Oksana Shulyak with Peter in the Romaniv isolation ward

Joining us in the class were Peter, an 11-year-old who was completely mentally healthy, but whose muscular dystrophy kept him confined to a wheelchair, and Dima, who had cerebral palsy, which affected his speech and movements, but not his mind. Because the uneducated and ill-equipped orphanage staff saw only these young men's physical limitations, they kept Peter and Dima in the isolation building, a place with zero mental stimulation. They spent almost all of their time in a place where nobody talked to them, nobody encouraged them, and nobody taught them anything. It was clear the MTU class was the absolute highlight of their week.

This should have been an uplifting moment for me. I should have been overjoyed at the love on display in front of me. But the more I sat there and thought about the ridiculously awful lives these boys were forced to live the other six days of the week, the more I felt hopelessness creeping into my heart.

I thought about the layers of injustice conspiring to keep this place a forgotten hellhole. Deep poverty, cultural stigmas towards disabilities, a profound lack of education, and years of neglect were like a witch's cauldron of brokenness that didn't seem to have any solution. Sure, it was great that MTU had begun to engage with the boys during their weekly visits, but let's be realistic here. What could a few hours a week *possibly* do to change the situation? Even if they had an unlimited budget, how could they combat such epic systems of injustice?

I wanted to *fix* Romaniv, but the more I looked, the more I realized that this was an impossible task.

And yet, these boys now had access to something they had never experienced before. They had friends who loved them. People who came to visit them in their distress. They had the hands and feet of Jesus sitting in their midst. So that's a great thing, right? Again and again, my mind spun these realities around. Injustice and hope. Pain and love. Death and life. It was like a dissonant chord in my heart, unsettling and unresolved.

At the end of the class, we packed up our things, walked into the crisp spring air, and made our way back to the van.

As we drove back to Zhytomyr, my head was reeling with all I had just seen and experienced. The cacophony of sounds echoed in my head. Images of boys' faces played like a slideshow. Even the smell stuck around, rubbed deep into the fabric of the clothes I was wearing. Meanwhile, the MTU team chatted like giddy schoolchildren about the experience. They were laughing and smiling and recounting all the little signs of progress they had seen in the boys.

Watching them celebrate like this left me stunned and speechless. The sheer compassion on display by the staff and volunteers from Mission to Ukraine was unreal. I could barely wrap my head around it. It wasn't just the fact that they *were* compassionate. It was *how* they lived out that compassion. When I looked at the Romaniv boys, I saw projects to be fixed. Problems to be solved. When *they* looked at the boys, they saw *people to be loved.*

This is why they were so excited on the way to the orphanage. *This* is why they were giddy as we drove away. While I was stewing on insurmountable obstacles and systemic injustice, they were basking in the glow of genuine love.

But here's the crazy thing; they had no idea this was anything special.

A few days after our visit, I wrote an article about Romaniv for World Next Door. I shared the story of my first visit and described the compassion of the MTU team in soaring and grandiose terms. From my vantage point, they were living out the kingdom of God in powerful, world-altering ways, and I said as much in my article. But they didn't see it. After reading my article, Oksana S came to me in tears and said, "I had no idea we were a part of something so big!"

This kind of selfless compassion was stunning, and it quickly become my new go-to picture of caring for the poor and marginalized. What I didn't realize at the time, however, was that the story of Romaniv was not over. There were still more mind-boggling revelations to come.

———

It was a beautiful summer day in 2010. More than a year had passed since my first visit to Romaniv. Once more I sat in a van hurtling through the Ukrainian countryside. Once more we dodged and weaved across the lanes in a death-defying display of vehicular insanity. This time, however, I had become rather desensitized to the danger. You can only grip the armrests so many times before your hands get tired. Besides, I hadn't died yet, so what was there to be afraid of?

A well-worn CD of Ukrainian worship songs played over the van's stereo system as we talked about our upcoming visit. My heart was filled with anticipation. I thought back to my unsettling, eye-opening, and life changing first experience, replaying memories of my first time meeting the boys.

I remembered the stench and the shrieks. I remembered my fear and uncertainty. But most of all, I remembered the inexplicably wholehearted compassion displayed by the MTU team.

I also wondered if there was anything tangible to show for their long obedience and consistent love. When I first visited, it was obvious that MTU's presence was having a huge impact on the boys themselves, but the orphanage was still a terrible, hellish place run by uneducated caretakers and filled with the stench of squalor. As we drove towards the orphanage this time, I wondered what, if anything, had changed.

As we got close to Romaniv, Oksana S turned to me and said, "Get ready. There is a big surprise waiting for you there!"

A surprise? I thought. *What in the world could she mean?*

I pondered this as we pulled up to the orphanage gate. We unloaded the van and started walking to the classroom building. That was when I did my first double take.

Flowers. Lots of flowers! Large, pink blossoms interspersed with yellow and red. Row after row of pretty blue blossoms lining the path. But that wasn't all. There were painted, rainbow colored benches. Between the buildings there were picnic tables with bright green canopies above them. This property, which once looked like an abandoned lot, now teemed with color and life. I was shocked.

Then we went inside, and my shock turned to utter amazement. There, on the floor of the once empty classroom was a semicircle of bright green and yellow desks. The walls that used to have only old wooden benches were now home to colorfully painted bookshelves overflowing with toys. In the corner of one classroom was a play-house with a window, a door, and a roof. Everywhere I looked I saw decorations and toys and stuffed animals. It looked like an actual classroom now!

But my amazement had only just begun. The smell, which was once bad enough to make me gag, was hardly noticeable now. The boys, once standing in puddles of urine, were now cleaned and dressed. And then came the kicker. As the boys sat down to begin their weekly class, it got *quiet*.

When Mission to Ukraine started coming to the orphanage two years before it was literally impossible for these boys to even form a line. They were out of control. Filthy.

Now, here they were sitting quietly, raising their hands when they wanted to participate, learning about the weather and doing the motions to their favorite songs. They took turns playing games, followed along as they learned a story from the Bible, and jumped in with shouts of joy when it was time for their favorite pastime: making bracelets out of beads.

Some of the young men at Romaniv sitting at their new desks

This was the surprise Oksana had for me. Romaniv had been transformed. At one point during the class, I pulled her aside, gestured to the desks and bookshelves and said, "This is amazing. Mission to Ukraine did all this?"

"No," she replied. "The orphanage administration did."

My jaw hit the floor so hard I thought I might need stitches. The *orphanage administration* bought these desks. The *orphanage administration* planted these flowers. The *orphanage administration* provided these toys. This was the same administration that once said the boys were essentially animals. The same people who didn't want MTU to come because they saw it as a waste of time.[3]

This was a twist I did not see coming. In their commitment to selfless compassion, Mission to Ukraine had begun to change an entire *system* of injustice. The kingdom of God, like a steady breeze, had been blowing away the smoke and the shadows in a place once filled only with hopelessness.

As we drove back to Zhytomyr that afternoon, I was stunned and humbled to have been a witness to such incredible change, but I also thought about the bigger picture. I thought about the other Ukrainian orphanages which have *not* yet had a transformation like Romaniv's. It's a thought I wrestle with to this day. The fact is, there are many more walls to smash down before the kingdom of God can truly shine in Ukraine.

But until that day comes, you and I can be confident of one thing: the staff of Mission to Ukraine will be there in Zhytomyr: hugging a girl with Down syndrome, wiping the chin of a boy with cerebral palsy, helping a girl with muscular dystrophy sit up straight in her chair, and tying a beaded bracelet for a boy at Romaniv.

They'll be there because they've tasted the kingdom of God. They'll be there because they've seen the hope of the gospel. And they'll be there because to the God they serve, nothing is impossible.

---

[3] A couple of years after this, the head administrator of the orphanage had even purchased gravestones for the boys who had died before MTU's visits. Until then they were simply buried in unmarked graves. Now, he saw their value as people.

2

Kibera

Shaving by lantern-light: cool and rustic the first time. Not so much the eighth.

I'm not going to lie. Moving into Kibera Slum for five weeks was terrifying. It was the very beginning of World Next Door in 2009 and I had no idea what I was doing. Even though I had visited Kibera several times before on previous trips to Kenya,[4] the prospect of actually *living* there filled me with apprehension.

Now, Kibera, one of the largest slums in East Africa, had been written about countless times by Westerners like me. The images of its endless sea of rusty metal roofs, muddy pathways, and sewage-filled streams were a dime a dozen online. The slum was huge, it was famous, and it was smack in the middle

---

[4] More on those other Kenya trips in later chapters. Like I said in the introduction, this book isn't in chronological order!

of Nairobi. There were about as many non-profits operating in the community as there were wildly inaccurate claims to its population size (most of which were based on a single guesstimate done by an aid organization in the early 2000's).

Unlike smaller, harder-to-reach slums in more dangerous sections of Nairobi, Kibera was only a five minute drive from Western-style malls and restaurants like Java House, where hungry Americans could get comfort food like hamburgers and quesadillas while connecting to reasonably fast free wi-fi. Because of its relative accessibility, Kibera had been the target of more missions trips, aid campaigns, and episodic acts of service than probably any other place in East Africa.

Kibera Slum's rusty metal roofs are iconic.

And yet, the slum didn't seem to be improving. No matter how much aid money got poured in, conditions only seemed to worsen. The slum only seemed to grow. Kibera was like a bottomless pit, swallowing up one aid organization after another. This phenomenon was illustrated by the vast number of abandoned clinics, half-finished elementary schools, and unused community centers built across the valley.

But even though working in Kibera had become somewhat cliché, I still trembled in my boots when I thought about making it my temporary home. First of all, there was the insecurity. From all the stories I had heard, lone *mzungus* (white people) like me were a major target for muggings, especially after dark. If I was *living* there, I'd be multiplying my chances of being robbed.

Then there was the disease. People living in Kibera got sick a lot. With questionable food, questionable water, and questionable *air*, my pansy American immune system wouldn't stand a chance. On top of that, there was the discomfort. I knew from earlier visits to my host ministry, Tumaini Church, that mud, sweat, rain, heat, and cold would all be factors I'd have to deal with every day.

Finally, I was scared to death of the people. I mean, everybody was kind and friendly and accommodating during my daytime visits, but how would they feel about an mzungu actually living in their world? Would I be welcomed as a guest or shunned as a poser? I worried my presence in the slum would be seen as an imposition, or worse, an offense.

The day I was scheduled to move into Kibera, I had two conversations with some of my Kenyan friends which set me even further on edge. One person said, "You're doing WHAT?!? That's crazy. You're going to get mugged." Another person said, "One of my friends was just in Kibera and he got *shot!*"

Great. Super encouraging, guys. Thanks.

After packing my bags, I grabbed lunch in a neighborhood just outside of Kibera called Hurlingham (presumably named after some kind of traditional pig-tossing competition). I ate a plateful of beef stew and rice, got out my journal, and wrestled with my fear. Just then, Romans 8:15 came to mind.

"For you did not receive a spirit that makes you a slave again to fear, but you received the Spirit of sonship."

I realized in that moment that my fear did *not* come from God. I was a son of the Creator of the universe. I was following a path he had set for me. What did I have to be afraid of? Clinging to that truth, I paid my lunch bill, grabbed my bags, and hopped on a *matatu* (public mini-bus) bound for

Kibera. I met Pastor Fred on the edge of the slum, and we walked into this new experience together.

———

Pastor Fred Faradays Ogutu and his wife Goretty were wonderful hosts. They even managed to provide me with my own tiny room for sleeping. It wasn't much. Just four walls, a chair, and a one-foot-wide path for walking around. But I was thrilled to have my own space in such an overcrowded community (the second time I lived in Kibera, two years later, I had to share a small bed with Fred's *brother* the whole time!).

Pastor Fred Faradays with his wife Goretty and sons Fortune (left) and Fadhili in 2011

Every night, I hung out with Fred, Goretty, and their sons Fadhili and Fortune in their small, 10 foot by 15 foot living room. We watched dubbed-over Mexican soap operas on their tiny TV and ate dinner with our hands. Our meals usually consisted of *ugali* (kind of like firm white grits), *sukuma wiki* (fried collard greens), and sometimes goat meat or scrambled eggs. It was all pretty standard fare for residents of the slum. Thankfully, the food, which I had found totally nauseating when I first visited Kenya, had actually started to grow on me.

One of the first things I noticed about living in Kibera was the constant noise. Because so many people were jam-packed in such a tight space, and because most homes were made of little more than tin, sticks, and mud, I could hear *everything* going on around me: mothers washing dishes, children laughing, a radio blaring, two men yelling, someone coughing, a dog barking, etc. It was a constant din in the background. This persistent noise led, of course, to frayed nerves on my part, but it was an important reminder of where I was and how little privacy the residents of Kibera enjoyed.

Because the slum was in the middle of a big, globalized city, its inhabitants were able to benefit from many conveniences of modern life despite the pervasive poverty of the place. The most obvious of these was electricity. I took it for granted immediately. For the first few days I charged my gadgets, used light switches, and watched TV pretty much whenever I wanted. That is, until the electricity stopped working for two days straight. As I quickly learned, power came and went a LOT in Kibera, and there was nothing anyone could do about it.

Sometimes a wire fell and it took the power company a while to get it fixed. Sometimes too many people tapped into the grid illegally and overloaded the system. Sometimes it hadn't rained in a while and Kenya's hydroelectric system came up short. And sometimes thugs dressed as electric company employees used ladders in broad daylight to steal expensive components like transformers, only to sell them back to the electric company through the black market a few days later. Whatever the case, it didn't take me long to realize power wasn't a dependable commodity (*hakuna stima*, or, "there is no electricity," was a Swahili phrase I picked up pretty quickly).

One evening after the power had been out for a few days, we were eating dinner by lantern light when the overhead lights and TV switched on unexpectedly. The power had been restored to our entire section of the slum. At that exact instant, I heard what seemed like hundreds of children shouting for joy. It was the stereotypical sound byte of excited children. "Yaaaaaayyyyy!!!!!!" With thin walls and open doorways, the restoration of power was a communal event.

Eventually I learned to live with a fickle power supply and other inconveniences like it. It took me quite a bit longer, however, to come to grips with the constant *discomforts* of life in Kibera. Things that would have once horrified me were now everyday occurrences. Mice darted under the couch while we were eating. Cockroaches crawled across the wall. And whenever it rained, my shoes and clothes got covered in mud. The day after I first moved in, I caught a nasty cold that had me sneezing and wheezing all over the place. One of the kids who saw me yelled out in amazement, "There is water coming out of the white man's nose!" It was the first of *many* colds and respiratory infections I picked up while living there.

To bathe, I had to wash myself using a bucket of water in what was essentially a bathroom stall. The four foot by eight foot closet had a hole in the ground which acted as both a toilet and a shower drain. Let's just say it wasn't an *ideal* situation for a germaphobic guy who generally had trouble touching handholds in the subway.

But this discomfort was where some of my most powerful learning experiences began. The more time I spent in Kibera, the more I realized I had no idea what it means to truly struggle. Everything I mentioned above – the mud, the overcrowding, the disease – these were all daily realities for the hundreds of thousands of people living there. Every day of every year for every person in the slum. These discomforts, when spread out over a lifetime, became ongoing tragedies that would be unspeakable for someone from my community back home: constant respiratory infections, unclean drinking water, children dying of preventable diseases. I had no idea what it was like to be at the mercy of such relentless injustice, but for the first time in my life, I had at least gotten a taste.

—

My discomfort was not just physical, however. As I spent more and more time in the slum, I felt less and less confident in my own abilities to effect change there. Where I once would have seen myself as a conquering hero with boundless potential to save the people of Kibera, I left the experience seriously wondering if I had *anything* to offer. All the skills and gifts I was so proud of suddenly seemed woefully ineffective against the relentless grind of injustice in that place. My cultural acumen was laughable, my understanding of poverty was childish, and my faith in God's provision was hollow.

You might think this would have led me to despair, but in fact the complete opposite was true. As I was awakening to my own limitations, I was also sitting at the feet of a tremendous leader who had a powerful capacity to change his community: Pastor Fred. My respect for the man grew more and more every day. As I saw him live out his calling in the slum, any question I had about where true community transformation would begin disappeared. Fred had rock solid faith, a deep understanding of poverty, and, as a Kenyan himself, a natural cultural awareness.

Fred was not a particularly imposing figure. His slender frame and gentle smile often camouflaged his blistering intellect and deep passion. After many long, profound conversations with the man, however, I threw all my preconceived notions about the idea of "a pastor in the slum" out the window. As you'll see from his multiple appearances in this book, Pastor Fred was one of a kind.

During my days in Kibera, I spent most of my time simply following Fred around. I went with him as he attended meetings, visited homes, led prayer gathering, etc. It was all pretty much normal pastor stuff (except most pastors I knew of back home didn't have to jump over streams of sewage to get to the home of an elderly congregant). I got to watch, firsthand, as God used Fred to touch the lives of many.

One instance, in particular, stands out in my memory. We were sitting in his small, dark office on the grounds of Tumaini Church. The sounds of the church's elementary school leaked through the walls. Pastor Fred was taking care of some paperwork when his phone rang. He answered, chatted for a few moments in Swahili, then hung up. He turned to me and said, "There is a child in the clinic. I am going to visit him. Do you want to come with me?" Since the prospect of an afternoon spent killing time in Tumaini's office all alone wasn't too attractive, I agreed.

We walked to the matatu stop on the edge of Kibera and took one of the cramped mini-busses to Nairobi West (an odd name for a neighborhood directly *south* of downtown Nairobi). At our stop we squeezed ourselves out of the crowded matatu and began walking down the bustling streets to a nearby clinic.

Nairobi, with its growing upper-middle class, thriving tourism industry, and large number of European expats, had quite a few modern medical facilities. They were clean, well-equipped, and effective. It also had a whole network of dark, filthy, woefully inefficient hospitals absolutely overflowing with people who couldn't afford decent treatment. The family we were visiting was part of Tumaini's congregation in Kibera. Needless to say, the clinic they were in was one of the latter.

I followed Fred up a flight of stairs and into the children's ward. Inside the long, narrow room was a row of beds. Every one of them was occupied by a sick child. The beds were separated by flimsy dividers, doing little to provide privacy for the family members huddled around the miserable children. Some of the mothers clutched plastic bags full of groceries. In Nairobi's lower-class clinics and hospitals, family members were responsible for providing their own food for the patients. A few of the children were covered in makeshift mosquito net tents, a last ditch effort to keep the child from contracting an even worse disease in the squalid conditions.

Passing by several dividers, we finally arrived at the bed of the child we had come to visit. He was about six or seven years old. Frail and obviously in pain, he lay on his side, clutching the hand of his mother, who sat next to the bed with a look of absolute helplessness on her face.

Pastor Fred began talking to the family in Swahili. He asked questions about the child's medical care, talked to them about practicalities like clinic fees, and spoke words of comfort and encouragement. At one point, he put his hand on the head of the child and told him how brave and strong he was. I could barely contain my emotions as I watched all of this transpire. I absolutely love kids, so seeing one in such a state of pain and desperation broke my heart in ways I can barely describe.

At some point, Fred turned to me and asked if I would pray for the child. My eyes grew wide.

"Uh, sure. Yeah," I said, wondering what I could possibly pray that would help this family.

I squeezed past Fred and found an empty spot next to the bed. I put my hand on the little boy's arm and started to pray. I got as far as "Heavenly Father…" before I burst into tears. I was sobbing uncontrollably. I didn't know the family. I didn't know the child, and yet I was overwhelmed with emotion at the tragedy of the situation. With access to modern medicine and a half-way decent medical facility, I had no doubt this child would be fine. But here, in this horrible, overcrowded place, his little body didn't stand a chance. And he was only one of *many* in just that room alone. I was a basket case.

Fred took over for me, praying for the boy's healing, for the family's strength, and for God's provision to meet their financial needs in this season. After the prayer, he said a few more words of encouragement to the family. When this was done, we reversed our earlier journey and made our way back to Kibera.

I spent the rest of the day in a funk. The emotions of the clinic visit had worn me down completely. Knowing the sick child's situation was absolutely *commonplace* was almost too much for me to bear. I was incapacitated and helpless in the face of so much poverty, and frustrated I had so little to offer. There was nothing I could do. I couldn't fix Kibera Slum.

But over the next few days, my despair began slowly transforming into hope. The more I thought about it, the more I realized that God was *not* absent in that place. In my powerlessness, I began seeing his handiwork everywhere I looked. I saw the Tumaini Church community coming together to meet each others' needs. I saw teachers and volunteers sacrificing much for the sake of their students' futures. Most importantly, I saw God raising up leaders who had something *powerful* to offer.

God was using people like Pastor Fred, whose compassion, perspective, and calling were infinitely more powerful in Kibera than mine could ever be. I knew Pastor Fred would be walking alongside the family of the sick child for many years to come. Meanwhile, Fred was hard at work raising up a whole *new* generation of leaders: young men and women on fire with dreams and visions of their community transformed.

Some of Tumaini Church's visionary young leaders.

Would the life-change they'd foster be evident immediately? Probably not. Would the injustices and poverty of Kibera be tackled once and for all? I doubt it. But would the kingdom of God continue its inexorable spread in that place through the brave and selfless leadership they were *born* to display? You'd better believe it.

———

In the end, after five transformative weeks living in Kibera (and another six weeks a couple of years later), I had had almost all of my preconceived notions about the slum get turned on their heads. First of all, I didn't get mugged or shot or killed even *once*. But more importantly, I had changed my perspective from one of despair to one of hope.

The hope in Kibera was not that I (or any Westerner) had deigned to offer it pity. The hope was that God was *already* on the move through the local Church. Humble, selfless leaders like Pastor Fred were displaying the love of Jesus with their lives, and *that* love is unstoppable!

3

The Path of Yes

---

*A great book title for an airport
bookstore self-help section*

When I first started traveling for World Next Door, I was stunned to encounter Christ-follower after Christ-follower living wildly sacrificial lives: working without a paycheck, sacrificing health, safety, and security for a greater mission, starting new initiatives with zero money in the bank, etc. At first, I couldn't believe my luck in coming across so many weird and extreme cases of faith. I felt privileged to have met such extraordinary followers of Jesus.

But over time, as these stories of incredible kingdom impact kept coming, I started to wonder if maybe I had it all backwards. I started to wonder if perhaps these Christ-followers were actually living "normal" lives of faith. I began to *redefine* what "normal" even meant. Maybe, I thought, these extreme people weren't so weird after all.

As I pondered all of this over my first few years of travel, I was also filled with a growing hope: Perhaps we in suburbia are *also* capable of living adventure-filled lives of faith. Maybe we, too, have the capacity to follow Jesus into a world-changing mission. Obviously, these "normal" Christ-centered lives may not look exactly the same as the lives of those in Kibera Slum or the mountains of Panama, but perhaps God has more in store for us than the bland, boring, *safe* lives we've been living.

It was an exciting concept. I began to imagine how tremendously transformed the suburbs of America would be if more and more Christ-followers began demonstrating the radical faith I had seen around the world: deep trust in God's provision, complete surrender to his purposes, and a powerful level of humility.

Of course, as I started to believe this was actually possible, it raised a pretty simple question. *How?* How does one even begin to live a world-changing life of faith? How do you become a *normal* follower of Christ? The answer, I now believe, lies in a word I've heard spoken many times by the amazing Christ-followers I've encountered around the world. It's a word they seem to be in the habit of saying loudly and often. The word is "YES."

It seems that every time God calls them to take a step of faith, their consistent, trusting answer is always the same: "Yes, Lord. I'll go." They don't ask questions. They don't raise concerns. They simply take the next step in their faith journey and God meets them along the way. I call the road they're walking the "Path of Yes."

In my friend Esperandieu Pierre's case, it started when he and his wife took a wrong turn outside of Port-au-Prince, Haiti. Trying to find the main road, they drove through the tiny, dusty village of Chambrun and saw something they didn't expect: extreme hunger, unbelievable poverty and a sight that made them sick to their stomachs: 13 year old girls breastfeeding their children.

Esperandieu, who grew up in a poverty-stricken community himself, had "won the lottery," so to speak, by receiving an international education. Coming back to Haiti after school, he had every opportunity to live high on the hog and ignore his hurting neighbors. But now the village of Chambrun had planted itself in his heart and he couldn't forget what he had seen. It was at this moment God asked the first question of Esperandieu: "Will you take a step of faith and use a small portion of your abundance to help the community of Chambrun?"

Esperandieu Pierre praying outside
Nehemiah Vision Ministries' clinic in 2010

Esperandieu and his wife decided to say "yes." They took a bit of money and helped open a small elementary school in the village. This "yes" led to another. They helped to start a children's home for kids without parents in the village. That "yes" led to another. That "yes" led to one more. And so on.

Each "yes" was a small step that led further and further into the unknown. Today, Esperandieu's organization, Nehemiah Vision Ministries (NVM), has grown into a multinational non-profit that is bringing hope and life to thousands of Haitians. The village of Chambrun is being transformed. But the really cool thing is that Esperandieu has never stopped saying "yes." When the 2010 earthquake struck, he once more stepped into the unknown and turned NVM into a conduit for thousands of volunteers, tons of supplies and millions of dollars of aid.

It all started with a single "yes." The first step of a journey. But because Esperandieu and his wife chose to turn that single yes into a lifestyle, *thousands* of lives have been transformed.

The story of my dear friend, Pastor Fred Faradays, is similar. Fred, who grew up in a small village in Western Kenya, was always very intelligent. Breaking free from the confines of rural poverty, he attended Bible school, where he graduated at the top of his class. It seemed as if Fred's life was destined to be one of success, comfort, and financial well-being. But God had different plans.

As Fred began his work in full-time ministry, he found himself deeply moved by the plight of young people living in Kibera Slum. He felt a strong call from God to use his skills and gifts to disciple these kids. Although he had every opportunity to advance, find a well-paying pastoral job at a big church, and settle into a life of plenty, he said "yes" to God and moved into Kibera instead.

This "yes" led to many others. Would he stay put in the midst of many obstacles? Yes. Would he marry and have children, knowing they would suffer in the slum? Yes. Would he start an elementary school, lead a church, and pursue community development projects with almost no money or support? Yes. It has not been an easy road for Fred and his family. Life in Kibera is harsh, painful, and uncomfortable. But Fred has been walking on the Path of Yes for decades, and today his life is a beacon of faith, hope, and love to many both inside and outside of the slum.

Of course, these two examples are from the developing world. The question still remains: is this even *possible* in the suburbs? What does it mean to walk along the Path of Yes when you're surrounded by SUVs, lattes, and big screen TVs? What about when you have children?

Well, consider the Elliott family for a moment. Aaron and Shelli Elliott are, in many ways, a somewhat ordinary suburban family. They have three kids, a dog, a green lawn, and a two car garage. But the journey they've been on for the last few years is anything but run-of-the-mill.

The Elliotts' first few steps along the Path of Yes included taking short-term trips to the developing world and financially supporting others who wanted to get involved. These first "yes" steps were a bit scary, of course (as are any steps into the unknown), but they were not particularly uncommon. However, they laid the foundation for much more challenging steps such as Aaron choosing to go into full-time ministry and their family deciding to adopt a child from Ethiopia.

The Elliott family in 2010

Then, on a short term trip to Haiti, Aaron and Shelli were asked to consider moving their family to Port-au-Prince for a year. It was a crazy idea, but they both felt God calling them to go. For the Elliotts, it was simply another step along the Path of Yes. Scary? Of course. Risky? Definitely. But for a family that had been saying "yes" to God for years, they knew it was the right thing to do.

They packed their bags, put their dog in a travel crate, and moved to the village of Chambrun. It ended up being a tremendous year in which God used their family in many ways to further the mission of Nehemiah Vision Ministries.[5] All because they said "yes."

As for me, I was a pretty average suburban kid most of my life. Fast food, video games, and comfort were the name of the game. But unlike the Elliotts, my own journey along the Path of Yes started in a much darker place. Instead of being asked to pursue something positive, I was asked to give something up. I had been attending Moody Bible Institute for three years when I first heard the call to take a step along the path. Although I went into my education at MBI with a deep passion for ministry, it had all but disappeared by my junior year. My own immaturity, my profound laziness, and the school's theology and philosophy of ministry (which were quite a bit more conservative than what I was used to) had all conspired to turn me into a cynical, angry mess.

Instead of pursuing my God-given passions, I spent my first three years at Moody obsessing over video games, procrastinating on my homework, and developing a taste for rebellion. Although I came into the school a straight-laced rule follower, it didn't take long for me to start breaking rules and delighting in my new identity as an "outsider." I was a rebel without a cause. But not the cool kind. The annoying kind. More like a rebel without a clue.

And then came Easter of 2004, towards the end of my junior year. I went home to Indianapolis with a few of my friends from school for my church's Easter service. Like good Bible school students should, we immediately came up with a list of all the things we didn't like about the service, all the "errors" we found in the sermon, and all the ways we would have done it differently. All of these things I innocently shared with my mother immediately after the service was over.

This might not have been a big deal if it wasn't for the fact that my father, the senior pastor of our church, was the one

---

[5] To read the full story of the Elliotts' year in Haiti, check out the book *In the Spirit of Nehemiah* by Aaron Elliott.

who had *given* the sermon and my mother, a professional pianist, had spent weeks beforehand helping to carefully design every aspect of the service. With no concern for the energy they had expended, I picked apart the service, complained about what I didn't like, then got in the car with my friends and headed back to school.

Me (second from left) with some of my college buddies
Freshman year. Also pictured: that haircut.

Now, the problem with this was not that I didn't like the service. The problem was not that I ignorantly assumed my biblical training was better than my father's, who had been a pastor for decades. No. The problem was that my words had deeply hurt my mother... and I had *no idea*.

For most of my life I have been a very empathetic person. I've always been hyper-aware of how other people are feeling. I'm not exaggerating when I say I get physically ill when my words or actions cause another person pain or embarrassment. So imagine my shock and surprise when my mom called a few days after Easter to tell me how much my words had hurt her. I had caused my mom significant pain and I hadn't even noticed. Of course I apologized profusely, but after hanging up I felt like I had been punched in the gut.

I immediately threw on my coat, headed outside and walked through the blustery streets of downtown Chicago to think through what all this meant.

"Who am I?" I asked myself. "What have I become?"

I was scared to realize that I had turned into a shadow of my former self. An empty shell of the person I was meant to be. No passion for ministry, annoyingly self-centered, and ignorant of how easily I had wounded someone I cared about deeply. I didn't like this version of me.

At the same time, I felt a simple but undefined tug from God to take a different path. Walking briskly through the chilly air, I knew I had a huge decision looming ahead of me. On one hand, I could continue down the path I had been treading for the last three years. I could head into my senior year, play more video games, graduate, and hopefully find some sort of job I didn't hate. Or I could take my first step onto the Path of Yes. I could quit school, step into the unknown, and trust that God would lead me somewhere good.

I'd be lying if I said it was an easy decision. Leaving my existing life behind was not a particularly attractive idea (it's called "the path of least resistance" for a reason). But by the time I had finished my walk, I knew what I had to do. I said "yes" to God and chose to take my first tentative step into the unknown. I finished the last month of my junior year, packed my things into my car, and quit school. My journey along the Path of Yes had begun.

The next six months were pretty rough. I worked at a coffee shop, lived in my parents' basement, and played lots and lots of video games. I sunk in and out of depression and wondered often if I had made a huge mistake.

Thankfully, my church had been in partnership with Nairobi Chapel, a thriving Kenyan congregation, for several years. The two churches had influenced each other in powerful ways, and had just started sending year-long interns back and forth. I had been considering the possibility of doing Nairobi

Chapel's internship after college, so I had at least one option to pursue. Now, let me be clear. Giving up video games and comfort and Mountain Dew for a year was *not* my idea of a good time. But I didn't want people to see me as a complete failure, so I needed to at least *look* like I had a plan. I dutifully filled out the internship application and sent it off to Nairobi Chapel. To my surprise, I got accepted. The second step on my Path of Yes was before me. Would I leave the comfort and security of home, spend a year away from my friends and family and risk the many unknowns of life in Kenya?

My answer was "yes," but barely. I really enjoyed being comfortable. I hated sweating. I was a very picky eater. This wasn't going to be easy. Ultimately, of course, I *did* get on the plane. It ended up being a *very* good call. Going to Kenya turned out to be the single most significant and life-changing decision I have ever made. I came out of the year far more mature than I was when I went in. My cynicism was replaced with hope and joy. My passion for ministry was rekindled. And my faith in God had never been stronger.

As my year in Nairobi drew to a close, my next step along the Path of Yes became clear. Would I return to Moody to finish up my senior year? Would I risk immersing myself in an environment that had sucked the life out of me before? Would I trust that God would use my newfound maturity to make me a source of life, not of darkness, to those I met there? I wasn't *entirely* sure it was a great idea, but considering how well the last two steps along the Path of Yes had gone, I decided to go for it. My answer was "yes." It ended up being a phenomenal senior year.

Since that day, I've taken quite a few more steps along the Path of Yes. Would I go to India for three months with no plan other than showing up and hanging out with Truthseekers? Yes. Would I start a photojournalism non-profit with absolutely zero training in photojournalism? Yes. Would I live in Kibera slum for five weeks? Yes. Would I live homeless in New York City for four days? Yes. Would I sleep in a Haitian tent camp? Yes. Each step has been slightly crazier and more intense than the one before, but each time God has come through for me in spectacular ways.

And this, for me, is the key to the whole concept. Walking along the Path of Yes does not take away the fear. All of the crazy things I've done over the last six years have been just as terrifying for me as you'd imagine. But looking back at the steps I've taken, I can see a clear track record of God's faithfulness. He has never let me down when I've trusted him enough to follow his call. So now, when I'm faced with a call from God that terrifies me, my confidence in his power and provision *far*, far outweighs my fear.

This, I believe, is the reason my "extreme" and "radical" friends around the world don't see their own lives as all that extraordinary. They've been on the Path of Yes for so long, they *know* God will always come through for them. So why let fear control their decisions? They've walked this path for years. They don't just *hope* mountains will move. They *expect* it.

I am confident this grand faith adventure is possible for every Christ-follower. Although it may not lead all of us to travel halfway around the world, taking the Path of Yes is possible for *anyone* willing to walk it. Who knows? If more of us start to say "yes" to God when he calls, perhaps even the suburbs of America will finally be home to more "normal" followers of Christ.

4

Spending Time

At least, I don't think she meant to spit on me.

I'm not sure what tipped me over the edge. It could have been the plastic seat handle digging into my back. It could have been hot dust blowing into my eyes. Maybe it was the baby vomiting all over the seat next to me.

Whatever it was, I had reached a special moment in my life: the most uncomfortable I'd ever been.

I was on a road trip to end all road trips. I was traveling to Lietnhom, a small village in the north of South Sudan, to see the work of a new World Next Door partner ministry, African Leadership and Reconciliation Ministries (ALARM). As a writer for World Next Door, I always did my best to understand what life was like for ordinary people in the places I visited. I had decided this time, for cultural immersion's sake (and because apparently I'm a glutton for punishment), to travel to Lietnhom *by land* instead of by plane. I had been told it would take a while, but thought, "How bad could it be?"

As it turns out? Pretty bad.

You see, the roads in South Sudan are not paved. Other than a few main streets in Juba and Wau, the country's roads are made entirely of dirt. But these are not some idyllic dirt roads through the countryside. These roads are malevolent. With giant potholes, massive rocks, and sharp drop-offs, they seem almost actively eager to swallow cars whole.

The trip, just over 350 miles, took 57 hours. Three *days* of travel.

But this was not spread-out-in-the-back-of-the-van-and-watch-movies-on-your-iPad travel. This was hold-on-for-dear-life-and-try-not-to-die travel. I flexed so much trying to keep my body upright I expected to have ripped biceps and six pack abs when we arrived.

But the worst part of this masochistic adventure was not the bag full of rotting bananas that spilled onto my leg. Nor was it the old lady who accidentally spit on my neck. It wasn't even the stench of 12 weary travelers crammed into a vehicle built for 7.

No. The worst part was that I could have flown. The fight takes an hour and a half. *And it costs the same amount.* Well, nearly the same. But when you add up how much misery could be spared from forking over just a tiny bit more cash, it seems like a no-brainer. Doesn't it?

As it turns out, it may not be so cut and dry.

———

My traveling companions for this epic journey were Magdelena, Josephine, and Kazito, students at the Christian Leadership Training Institute (one of ALARM's initiatives in South Sudan). They were traveling to their homes in Lietnhom at the same time as my trip, so they graciously offered to let me join them.

During one long, nauseating stretch of road, I brought up the cost difference to them. My new friends wrote it off immediately.

"Flying costs much more than driving," they told me.

"Yeah! But not if you add up the other expenses!" I argued.

"Yes, but the flight costs more," they replied.

A bit frustrated, I pulled out my notebook and started writing figures. My handwriting was made nearly illegible by the jostling of the vehicle.

"So it costs 80 pounds to get from Yei to Juba by road. And then, what, 400 to reach Wau?" My traveling companions agreed. I continued my tally. "Plus 60 to reach Lietnhom. But going by road means you have to spend the night in two locations. 40 pounds a night, right? And let's say 50 pounds for food."

How many passengers can you fit inside a
South Sudanese Land Rover? One more.

My final count came to 670 South Sudanese Pounds (SSP). To the right of this column, I tallied up what it would cost to fly instead. The total ended up at 760 pounds.

In other words, the difference in cost was only 90 SSP (less than $30 US), but by flying, the trip was shorter *by two full days.*

To me, this was an easy decision. Of *course* $30 would be worth two days of my life. I said as much to my friends.

Magdalena turned to me and repeated, "Yes, but flying is more expensive."

At first I was baffled. Was she missing the point I was trying to make? Did she not see the simple "90" circled in my notebook? How is that not worth it?

I asked Kazito what he thought, and he told me, "Of course we would love to fly. This trip is too difficult. But the money is too much."

That's when I began to understand just how differently my friends and I saw that $30. And how differently we saw the value of our time. I chewed on this concept a lot as the trip wore on. The ride was so bumpy that reading was impossible, so I simply stared out the window for hours on end.

As an American, I reflected, I tend to believe the concept that "time is money." I talk about "spending" time and "wasting" time. I say things like, "Can I steal a second of your time?" and "Can I borrow you for a minute?" Time is a commodity for me, and it's reflected in the way I use my money.

I'll pay a bit more for a shorter flight. I'll drop a few dollars to have my car washed in a drive through. I'll even pay a bit of extra cash for faster Internet so I won't have to wait for YouTube clips to buffer.

Time is money.

But what if I didn't *have* money? What if poverty took away my option for speeding things up? What if 30 extra dollars was an expense I simply couldn't afford?

Well, then I guess I'd travel to Lietnhom by ground and suffer through three long, agonizing days for a trip that should have taken less than one. Which is exactly what my traveling companions chose to do.

When you are living in poverty, I realized, time and comfort *have no value*. They are expendable. And you really have no choice in the matter.

Needless to say, this got me pretty down. Realizing that "the most uncomfortable I'd ever been" was *normal life* for a huge portion of humanity was a sobering experience, to say the least.

But then something interesting happened. We reached Lietnhom, and I discovered a silver lining to this dark cloud.

In the village of Lietnhom, life moves pretty slowly.

Because of the intense heat, people often sit around for long stretches of the day. I spent much of my time sitting in chairs, listening to people chitchat, and drinking chai. To be honest, I didn't feel particularly industrious.

But I soon realized this sitting around wasn't just idleness. People in Lietnhom visit each other's homes. They enjoy long, comfortable conversations with each other. Nobody ever rushes off to a meeting and nobody ever gets concerned when someone is running late.

While I was stirring anxiously in my seat, wondering when the person I was meeting would show up, my South Sudanese friends were laughing and enjoying each others' company.

That's when it began to dawn on me. Sure, when poverty removes the value from your time, it can lead to some pretty uncomfortable situations. But it also opens the door to something beautiful. When time isn't a commodity you have to protect, when it's not an investment constantly eating away at you, it loses its power to control you.

Perhaps this was a lesson I needed to learn. Maybe I hold on to time a bit too closely. Maybe my life would be richer if I tried to be more "present" when I was with people instead of constantly checking the time. Maybe some of the stress I feel day to day is self-imposed.

As I left Lietnhom a few days later, I looked forward to *flying* back to Juba. The trip that took me three days one way would take less than *one* on the return journey. But instead of looking at that "saved" time as a commodity to re-invest, I found myself thinking of it as a gift.

As I stepped off the plane in Juba and thought about what I'd do the rest of the day, the question wasn't, "How will I *spend* my time?" but "Who will I share it *with*?"

5

The Banya

Birch trees still make me flinch.

I stood on the damp tile floor in my boxers, shivering in the chilly spring air. In my hand was a mug full of kvass, a traditional Ukrainian drink that tasted an awful lot like liquefied rye bread. I took a gulp, tried not to gag, then smiled at Taras, my host brother and interpreter during my first visit to Zhytomyr. I didn't want him to realize how far out of my comfort zone I was just then.

We were about to "go to banya," which nobody had really explained to me. From what I could piece together, it sounded like some kind of sauna. Except every time I mentioned "going to banya" to my new Ukrainian friends, they got big, mischievous grins on their face, wished me *luck*, then chuckled as if I was about to be the target of a dorm room prank.

I took another mouth full of kvass. Seriously gross. I didn't even like rye bread in *bread* form. But at least I wasn't being rude to my hosts. As I swallowed, I looked over at the huge glass jar full of animal bits marinating in a cloudy brown liquid:

something called *shashlik*, our dinner after banya was over. It reminded me of an artifact you might find in the lab of some mad scientist. For someone who was once nauseated by the sight of a bone in a chicken wing, I was just a *bit* in over my head.

I looked over at Taras, who was staring intently at a thermometer next to a wooden door, the entrance to the banya.

"Oh, good," said Taras. "They've made it nice and hot."

I walked over and looked at the thermometer. "80 degrees," I observed. "That will really feel nice."

"Yes," Taras replied. "80 degrees Celsius is perfect for banya."

"Wait," I said. "80 degrees *Celsius*? That's like... 180 degrees Fahrenheit!!!"

Uh oh, I thought. Before I had a chance to reconsider the wisdom of what I was about to do, it was time. Taras opened the door and we shuffled in to a tiny wooden shack with a metal stove in one corner, and benches lining the walls. It was HOT. My nostrils were immediately singed. I had trouble breathing. Shocked by the onslaught of extreme heat, I looked up to see who else would be suffering with us. Staring down at me from one of the benches was a shriveled, sweaty, half-naked Ukrainian octogenarian.

He gestured angrily in my direction, "Zakryy dveri!"

Taras quickly translated, "Close the door!"

I closed the door.

It didn't take long for me to learn that Ukrainian banyas *are* like saunas. On steroids. When men "go to banya," they *do* like to relax, sweat out their stress, and have enlightening conversations. They *also* like to drink vodka, beat each other with birch branches, and make stupid decisions like jumping into freezing rivers.

On this, my first of many banya experiences, there was no alcohol, but the manliness, madness, and masochism were very much intact. After "enjoying" our first sweat in the small wooden shack, the men in our group took turns in the banya for what I can only describe as friendly, good-natured *torture*. Since Taras was the only English-speaker in the group, I had to face the pain with absolutely *no* idea what was going on.

A man I had never met before gestured for me to lie down face first on one of the benches. I lay on my stomach, trying not to bump my feet or elbows into the scorching hot wall. Out of the corner of my eye, I could see the man ladling some water onto the rocks surrounding the stove. Immediately, the entire room filled with thick clouds of steam, and I found myself choking, practically unable to breath the hot, humid air.

Next, the man took a large bunch of leafy birch branches out of a bucket of water, flicked more droplets on the hot rocks, and then began shaking the leaves over my back. Words cannot describe just how intense the heat became. It was like someone opened an oven immediately above my body. Somehow, the moving air and moisture *multiplied* the pain.

I let out an audible groan, absolutely convinced that it couldn't get any worse. That's when the man started beating me. He shook the leaves over my legs and back, then just started wailing on me with them.

Shake. Shake. Shake. SLAP. Shake. Shake. Shake. SLAP.

This went on for a few agonizing minutes. Then he gestured for me to flip over so he could continue the torture on my front side. When it was finally over, the man walked out of the banya, and I staggered behind, eager to get away from the extreme heat. I walked out the door, turned the corner, and was immediately doused with a bucket of ice cold water by a smiling Taras.

This was the beginning of banya. For the next hour and a half, we rotated in and out of the wooden shack, sweating like mad, beating each other, and getting doused by freezing water. To my great surprise, I found myself absolutely loving the experience. As much as it hurt, banya was a *blast*.

When we had finally had enough, we showered off, dressed, then shuffled outside. Yuri, Taras' dad, lit a fire and began roasting skewers of the marinated meat. We looked up at the stars, laughed about the insanity of banya, and ate what turned out to be some of the most delicious meat I had ever tried. At about one in the morning, we got in the car, drove home, and crawled into our beds to sleep like the dead.

I had "gone to banya," and survived.

6

Encounters

I have better luck than Mufasa, apparently.

So here's a reasonable question. How exactly does a picky-eating, comfort-loving, video-game playing suburban kid end up starting a world-traveling photojournalism non-profit and spending six years living in slums, refugee camps, and mountain villages?

That's a great question. I have no idea.

But this is how it happened for me.

It all started back in 2005 when I was living in Nairobi, Kenya for my year-long internship with Nairobi Chapel. As I said before, I had a time getting myself there. Before leaving home, my imagination ran wild with images of wildebeest stampedes, intestinal parasites, uncontrollable sweat, and, worst of all, *no Xbox*. I mean, Halo 2 had just come out. How was I supposed to go an *entire year* without playing it? To make a long story short, I somehow, miraculously, got myself on the plane and ended up living in Kenya for a year.

It turned out to be the best decision of my entire life.

During my internship with Nairobi Chapel, I went through a crazy number of changes physically, emotionally, mentally, spiritually… you name it. I lost 15 pounds, I replaced a lot of my nervous energy with focus, I started eating new foods, etc. It was a time of transitions for me.

One of the biggest of these changes, though, was a heightened understanding of my own brokenness. For the first time in my life, I was disconnected enough from "the old me" to see just how broken and sinful and messy I really was. Separated from my old house, my old friends, my old habits, and my old routines, I got to the core of who I was… and didn't like what I saw.

As I came to grips with that unsettling fact, I made a decision that would forever alter the course of my life. I decided to confess every un-confessed sin in my life to the people who knew me best: my parents.

(No. I don't know what I was thinking either.)

We arranged an international phone call and I poured out all of the junk I had been bottling up inside. And as awkward as it is to have my mom know every un-confessed sin from my middle school years, I left the call feeling unbelievably free.

With this concrete acknowledgement of my own brokenness out in the open, the stage was set for three "encounters" with God that would ultimately lead me to my first true understanding of my calling.

—

The first of these three encounters with God came towards the end of my time in Kenya. In late 2005, I found myself sitting around a bonfire with a group of new Kenyan believers. They were about to graduate from a ten-week discipleship class I had helped to lead.

Pastor Muriithi and Pastor Simon (two of the pastors I had the privilege of working under) led a debriefing time for the group. They had each member share how they had changed during the class, then got up to lay hands on everyone and pray a blessing over them. One by one, the class members walked up to one of the pastors and received a prayer.

My church background isn't particularly charismatic, so you can imagine my surprise when one of the people being prayed for called out in a loud voice, fell over backwards and started mumbling in tongues on the ground. I had never seen anyone "slain in the Spirit" before, so this experience was a bit, well, startling.

As I stared, wide-eyed, wondering what in the heck was going on, another person fell over in the exact same way. My heart was pounding. Just then, Pastor Simon leaned over and asked, "Barry, can you please stand behind people so that they don't fall into the fire?"

"Um… sure?"

This night was turning out to be a bit more interesting than I had expected. By the time I had caught the third person falling in a swoon and helped them to the ground, I was ready for just about anything. If a couple of flying muskrats had jumped out of the fire and started singing Christmas carols, I would have been like, "OK then."

Thankfully, there were no flying muskrats. Only person after person deeply moved by the Spirit. Person after person having an emotional and transformative encounter with God.

Then it was my turn.

"Can I pray for you, Barry?" asked Pastor Simon.

"Sure," I said, wondering just what I was getting myself into. "I guess so."

As I stepped up to Pastor Simon, I braced myself and took a wide stance. I was not about to fall over. No thank you. *You can pray for me,* I thought, *But I am sticking with English tonight.*

Instead of simply praying, however, Pastor Simon shared a prophecy with me. Again, not a normal thing for me back home.

"Barry, the other day God gave me a vision for you. I saw you as a bowl full of fruit. Many people were coming around and eating their fill. Everyone was laughing and filled with joy."

I stared, wide-eyed, as Pastor Simon continued.

"Barry, I believe God is going to use you to bring life and joy to many people. He has big things in store for you." After saying this, Pastor Simon put his hands on my shoulders and prayed over me.

When he was finished, I thanked him and wandered into the darkness away from the bonfire. I leaned up against a tree and began reflecting on what I had just experienced. The prophetic image kept appearing in my head. Bearing fruit and bringing joy to others. God using me to bring life to this world.

Then, out of nowhere, I remembered the huge laundry list of un-confessed sins I had shared with my parents a few months before. I remembered my countless weaknesses, my overwhelming insecurities, and my unending patterns of sin.

Within seconds, I was weeping. *God wants to use me?* I thought. *Why? I'm a mess. A broken, weak, powerless mess.* I closed my eyes, wiped the snot from my face and asked God that simplest of questions, "Why me?"

The answer I received was not audible, but I felt it in every fiber of my being.

"Because you are my son."

That was all I heard from God, but that was all I needed to hear. In those five little words, the prophecy, my brokenness, my year in Kenya, my shortcomings, and God's heart for the world fused into a single idea that put its roots deep into my heart: "God wants to use me for his purposes. Not when I'm perfect. Not when I've got it all figured out. God wants to use me *now*. Brokenness and all."

It was the first time I really understood the concept of grace.

—

Needless to say, this experience stuck with me. As terrified as I was going in, my year in Kenya was the best thing that had ever happened to me. Oh, and wildebeest stampedes weren't even that much of a factor after all.

I went back to finish up my last year of college instilled with a new sense of purpose, drive, and vision. God wanted to use me. *I was a fruit basket!* And I was going to do everything in my power to make that prophecy a reality.

It was then, during my senior year of college, that the

second encounter took place. At Moody Bible Institute, it's a tradition for the whole senior class to get away for a weekend and to have a "Senior Retreat" together. It's a time, as you might expect, full of many "reach for your dreams" speeches and tearful reminiscing about the past four years. The only problem, of course, was that I hadn't *been* there for the last four years. I had been gone from school for the last two, meaning that everyone I celebrating senior year with was a freshmen when I left.

Oh well. Free hot dogs.

God must have a sense of humor, though, because it was *there* that I got hit upside the head with number two of my crazy-encounters-with-God-that-launch-me-into-the-next-stage-of-discovering-my-calling-even-though-the-steps-he's-asking-me-to-take-are-kind-of-terrifying-but-it's-OK-because-he-seems-to-know-what-he's-doing experiences.

We were singing some worship song. The dude up front was strumming away at his guitar. The PowerPoint girl had just switched over to the mountain, waterfall, and eagles background. Key change.

When boom. Out of nowhere my mind was overwhelmed with a rapid slideshow of poverty. Specifically the poverty I had seen in Nairobi. Sewage filled streets. Endless slums. Kids with distended bellies staring at me. Bam. Bam. Bam. One image after another.

Before I knew what was happening, I was sobbing. Seriously, shaking as I wept. The people around me looked at me like I was out of my mind. I mean, the worship set wasn't *that* powerful.

I stumbled out of the room and found the nearest bathroom. I washed my face and looked at myself in the mirror.

"This isn't an option anymore," I thought. "Poverty, hunger, AIDS... These aren't just things I can care about when I have a little bit of extra time or money. Caring for the poor and marginalized has *got* to be central to my faith. Not just something I tack on at the end."

It's a bit embarrassing to admit that it took me eight months after returning from Kenya to realize this, but it had finally happened. I knew I couldn't go back again. Justice and mercy were now central to my life, whether I liked it or not.

There was only thing I needed to figure out: what in the *world* did that even mean?

———

After graduating from college, I decided to explore this question through *another* year-long internship, this time at my home church on the north side of Indianapolis. I worked with the Outreach team and got my feet wet connecting suburban people to issues of social injustice for the first time.

This was when I began to notice a unique skill that I seemed to have. I could talk to latte-drinking, TV-buying, SUV-driving suburbanites about issues of global poverty without making them feel judged. For some reason, people listened to me without putting up their usual walls of apathy, indifference, and annoyance.

I got excited. I felt like I was finally stepping into a role that fit my gifts and passions. Working at a church and pastoring people into kingdom relevance. I had found it!

And then every door slammed in my face.

As my internship drew to a close, I started applying to any job that even remotely resembled what I thought I was meant to do. A church here. A ministry there. And every response I got was the same: "No experience."

I wasn't exactly thrilled with God at that moment. "Really?" I asked him. "You're going to take me through all of that and then just drop me on my butt? What am I supposed to do now?"

No answer. Nothing.

Until one night, in the midst of my frustration, when my parents invited Sunil and Pam Sardar over to their house for dinner. Sunil was the leader of Truthseekers, a ministry in India that seeks to end the oppression of the Caste System through the power of the kingdom of God.

As we were sitting in the living room chatting, Sunil looked straight at me and said, "Barry, you should come to India for three months. Don't worry about food or shelter. We'll take care of you. Just show up."

As crazy as that sounded, I had nothing else going on, so I said, "OK, why not?" I scraped together enough money for a ticket, said goodbye to my family and friends and boarded a plane bound for New Delhi.

When I reached the airport, I hadn't met any of the people who would be picking me up. I just knew someone probably would. As I walked up the ramp out of the terminal, however, I started to lose confidence. All I saw was a seemingly endless sea of dark haired, mustachioed men holding signs. I searched and searched until I finally saw a sign that said, "Bany Rodgmanez."

I looked at the smiling men holding the sign and asked, "Truthseekers?"

They replied, "Yes! Sunil!" and beckoned me to get in their car.

I nodded, smiled, and took a seat in their vehicle. Moments later, we were tearing into the evening traffic of New Delhi.

For the next three months I hung out with the leaders of Truthseekers. I attended anti-discrimination rallies, sat in the homes of outcast eunuchs, visited schools built for gypsy children, and slogged through the mud in rural Maharashtra. I had some pretty unique cultural experiences as well. I took 22-hour train rides by myself, explored crowded markets, and even tried goat brains for the first time. Meanwhile, I was reading stacks of books about the caste system and the history of India. I was learning a *ton*. It was an amazing trip.

The whole time I was there I felt compelled to share what I was learning and experiencing on my blog. Some posts were funny and weird. Others were heartfelt and intense. All of them were geared toward my readers: suburban American Christians.

That's when I discovered something interesting. People who read my blog posts were saying more than just "Hmm. Interesting article," or "Thanks for sharing." They were saying things like, "That post changed the way that I see the world," or "I'm going to get involved with Truthseekers financially now." Somehow, by experiencing the kingdom of God in India and sharing these stories online, I was helping suburban Americans get engaged with social justice issues. I had stumbled into a means of accomplishing my calling just by doing what I now loved to do.

That is when I had my third "encounter" with God. Halfway through my time in India I called my dad to chat about what was happening. During our conversation, he casually said, "Wouldn't it be cool if you could do this full time?"

Boom. A light bulb went off in my head. Yes. It would be *very* cool if I could do this full time. I loved to travel by that point, I was a decent writer and, most importantly, unengaged suburbanites seemed to listen to me.

I had found it. The means to live out my calling. I would travel. I would write. And I would use my articles and influence to wake up suburban America and change the course of injustice in our world!

There was only one problem. I had no idea what I was doing. But details, details… I was sure I'd figure it out.

7

Hospitality of
the Heart

I really was fine sitting on the ground.

I awoke to the sound of a baby crying. Covered in sweat, my feet itching from a thousand mosquito bites, I sat up and looked around. In the dim, pre-dawn light, I could make out the sleeping body of my interpreter, Denis.

Over his right shoulder lay Pierre Moise, Kenchise, Williamson, and Ismail. Their mother, Laneze, slept on a blanket just outside the tent flap. Beyond her was Presilma, the father of the family, sitting up with his arms wrapped around his knees, rocking slightly back and forth. I was surprised to see another person awake so early, but as I listened carefully to the soft words coming from Presilma's direction, I understood. He was praying.

It was my third visit to Haiti, and I was in the middle of a completely unbelievable experience. I had the privilege to spend a week and a half living in one of the internally displaced people (IDP) tent camps with a family of Haitian earthquake refugees, the Dazmas. Like millions of other Haitians, the Dazmas' home had been destroyed in the 2010 earthquake. A series of small miracles kept them out of harm's way while the building collapsed, but they had little to celebrate now that their entire family had been living in a tent for six months.

The Dazmas' new home was a tent community called Dadadou. Before the earthquake it was a soccer field. Now it had become a hot, crowded, bustling pile of tents, housing over 10,000 refugees. Other than the running track, which had become a sort of makeshift "main street," every square inch of the property was covered with tents. Let's just say it was crowded. And I was another warm body thrown into the mix.

Dadadou tent camp

Day-to-day life in Dadadou seemed to oscillate between life-threatening chaos and a new kind of normal. For example, the Dazmas barely had enough food to eat. My heart broke one morning as I watched the children eat small handfuls of cassava (a potato-like root vegetable), knowing their only other meal for the day would be dinner - a plateful of rice and beans topped with a small portion of mackerel.

And yet, in the midst of this hardship, Presilma (the father), daily headed back to his old neighborhood to work. He was a tailor, and although there was very little business those days, he had no choice but to set up shop in the hopes that a customer or two might come along. Denis and I visited him at work a couple of times. Presilma's tailor shop was on the ground floor of the building in which his family used to live. Their ruined apartment was on the third floor. As he worked, friends and neighbors would stop by to visit and chat. Occasionally his kids swung by on their way to visit cousins down the street. If it wasn't for the fact that they were living in a tent and clinging desperately to the bottom rung of extreme poverty, you would think the Dazmas were back to life as usual.

As I watched the family through the many *un*eventful moments in their lives, I developed a deeper picture of the life they were now living. Although they had settled into a sense of normalcy in their day-to-day routine, I could feel the stress of their situation brimming just under the surface.

For example, one afternoon, as the youngest of the Dazma kids were taking cover from the mid-day sun, I sat and watched them play jacks with a few stones. This would have been a totally ordinary image from any number of places around the world except for one thing: the only shade they could find was a tiny alley between two tents.

Every few minutes, their mother would step over them, taking pots and pans back and forth from the charcoal stove she was using to cook dinner. To keep the tent from burning down, she had to use the stove out in an open area about 30 feet away from her makeshift kitchen. It was obviously a major hassle.

For a short time, I thought, inconveniences and discomforts like these can be overlooked. But how long can someone really live in a home where they can't even stand up straight?

One evening we were sprawled out on the ground behind their tent, enjoying the evening breeze. The Dazmas' "back yard," for lack of a better term, was a 15' x 15' square formed by neighboring tents. The ground of the soccer field was made of Astroturf, so it made an ideal place to hang out once the sun went down.

But even in this moment of respite from the heat, I could see how their situation was taking a toll. The Dazma's neighbors had a rambunctious two year old boy. His recklessness and inquisitiveness was always good for a laugh. However, in the evening, when his energy started to disappear, he inevitably turned into a whining, crying mess.

Anyone in the world who has had a two year old will tell you that he/she can sometimes bring out less than the best in a family. Patience wears thin, tempers flare, frustrations can't be covered over any more. But in Dadadou, these moments of everyday family strife cannot be hidden away. There we were, sitting three feet outside of their neighbor's tent, seeing and hearing everything that was going on. I saw the dirty looks and tense body language. I heard the anger and the arguments. When thousands of people live in such close proximity, there is no such thing as "airing your dirty laundry." It's already out there for the world to see.

The Dazma family and me outside their tent

Every day I saw more and more mundane details that revealed the pain, stress, and fear that lay just below the surface in Haiti's many IDP camps. These weren't the food riots and disease outbreaks you might have heard about on the news. These were not the massive protesting crowds. These were the simple, day-to-day struggles of people living on the brink.

And yet, the Dazmas seemed to be cut from a different

kind of cloth. The tension and simmering rage lying just below the surface of so many seemed completely absent from their family. They were full of joy and life. Every morning, Presilma got up before the break of day to pray for his family's well being. Every day he washed his face and headed off to work. Every time I saw him, I was greeted by a bright smile and a firm handshake. The kids were happy and helpful. Laneze, the mother of the family, seemed endlessly peaceful and calm. And to my complete surprise, they were genuinely some of the most hospitable people I had ever met.

My first glimpse of this unexpected hospitality came after Denis and I had been in the Dazmas' tent for only a few minutes on our very first day. After sitting and chatting for a while, Laneze, the mother of the family, jumped up and busied herself on the other side of the tent. When she came back, she had in her hand a giant, steaming plate of rice and beans, much more than either Denis or I could possibly eat. We thanked her for her generosity but insisted that we split the plate between the two of us.

It was a tasty meal, but it wasn't until later that I realized how significant that small gesture really was. I hadn't yet learned about the Dazmas' financial situation. I didn't realize their minuscule budget usually gave them only enough to provide one meal a day for their kids. The whole family struggled with malnutrition, and yet there they were, providing an enormously generous meal to their guests. Wow.

But it didn't stop there. When we realized that the Dazmas were going to be feeding us regularly, I quickly made the decision to give them money to cover the cost of food. Denis agreed that it was a good idea, but told me, "We'll need to make sure they don't buy a chicken for us." At first I was a bit confused about what he meant. Then it dawned on me. Denis knew that because the Dazmas were so generous, once they had a few *gourdes* (Haiti's currency) in hand they would immediately go out and blow it all on fancy meals for their guests! When we did end up giving the money to Laneze, we had to insist that she feed us whatever they would *normally* eat instead of an expensive chicken dinner.

She actually needed convincing.

Another aspect of their unexpected hospitality came from their almost fanatical dedication to my comfort and security. Even the little things – the seemingly inconsequential details – pointed to a hospitality rooted deeply within their family.

When it came time to set up our small air mattresses our first evening there, they insisted we sleep inside the tent to stay out of the rain. Presilma and Laneze, we understood, would be perfectly happy to sleep under the tarp outside. I felt awful being such an intrusive presence, but every time I offered to make a sacrifice for *their* comfort, they wouldn't hear of it.

Every time they saw me sitting on the ground, one of the Dazma kids would run up with their family's single wooden stool to make sure I was comfortable. When I was walking through town with their oldest son Ismail, he pointed out every pothole, rock or crack in the sidewalk that might have caused me to stumble. When I yawned in the evening, they asked me, "Are you tired? You can sleep now if you'd like." And of course, five minutes later I would discover that our air mattresses had been laid out neatly in the corner of the tent.

Obviously the Dazmas wanted to take good care of their guests. But there was another, even deeper kind of hospitality I discovered while living with the Dazma family: hospitality of the heart. It made me re-think the whole concept of generosity.

Throughout my time with them, the Dazmas were remarkably honest and open with me about their lives. They let me enter into the center of their family's day-to-day existence. They exposed the potentially shameful truth that they do not have enough to get by - an especially significant thing in a culture like Haiti's. They also risked all sorts of unknown consequences by having a *blan* (white person) stay in their tent. What would their neighbors think? What if some unruly men in the community decided to start making trouble? What if the *blan* embarrassed them? Despite all the potential outcomes, their hearts were open. They welcomed a stranger into their home - one of the purest forms of hospitality I can think of.

And that's the truly mind-blowing thing about all of this. In Matthew 25, Jesus says to those on his right, "I was a stranger and you invited me in" and "whatever you did for one of the least of these brothers of mine, you did for me." Is it possible that, to the Dazmas, *I* was one of the "least of these?"

Boom. Mind blown.

My entire stay in Dadadou was turned upside down because of the incredible hospitality of my hosts. The tables were turned in ways I never could have expected. The Dazmas were living, breathing representations of the body of Christ. That was the common thread in all of this. Their endless patience, their inexplicable joy, their overflowing generosity - these were all made possible because they followed Jesus.

I never thought I'd receive a lesson in hospitality while living in a refugee camp, but thanks to the Dazma family, I'll never think of 'loving my neighbor as myself' in the same way again.

8

Tea Time

It's a great thing I'm not lactose intolerant.

If there's one thing people in Kenya love, it's chai. A clear holdover from British colonial rule, drinking cup after cup of sweet, milky tea is the *sine qua non* of every social gathering. While I was living with Pastor Fred in Kibera Slum, we drank two cups in the morning, one in the afternoon, and one more at dinner - *as a baseline.* That was the minimum on busy days working in the Tumaini Church office. When we were doing *home visits*, however, the cups of chai per hour (or CCPH) skyrocketed.

Each home visit was very similar. Pastor Fred and I would show up in a family's tiny, ten foot by ten foot home, and sit on whatever chairs or couches they had perched around their coffee table. Sometimes this was after being invited over. Sometimes it would be an unexpected visit. Either way, we'd always be welcomed warmly. The point of these visits was to pray for and encourage families of Tumaini Church and its neighbors, but each stop inevitably turned into a social event.

Looking back, I suppose this makes sense, since Kenyans are generally *very* hospitable. Even within a slum like Kibera, families would feel ashamed to have guests without offering them tea.

The visits followed a predictable pattern. Moments after Pastor Fred and I took our seats, the mother of the family would jump up, go to the other side of the room, and start boiling water for chai. Within just a few minutes, we'd have hot tea with milk, a large bowl of sugar, and slices of white bread spread with margarine laid out in front of us. To honor the hospitality of our hosts, we *had* to drink at least one cup of tea and eat at least one slice of bread. Taking another cup was always a polite gesture. Often, after visiting four or five homes in a row, I'd be shaking from an overdose of sugar and caffeine, needing to pee like a racehorse, and feeling sick to my stomach from eating essentially a full *loaf* of white bread (a phenomenon I think I'll call "loafin' it.").

In those moments, loafin' it with a sustained CCPH of more than 5, it was hard to believe there was *ever* a time in which I was a social pariah in that community. But that's exactly how my time in Kibera began.

OK. Perhaps "pariah" is a bit strong, but imagine my surprise when I first moved into Kibera and *never* got invited over for chai. Two full weeks went by with almost nobody from the Tumaini Church congregation opening up their home. I didn't say anything about it to Pastor Fred at the time, because I had no idea what was really going on. Were people there too poor to buy tea? Was I unaware of some social dynamic affecting their hospitality? Was it something I said?

As it turns out, it wasn't that nobody wanted to host me. It was that nobody wanted to be the *first* person to host me. Pastor Fred explained to me that many *mzungus* (white people) come to Kibera with grand agendas, plans, or initiatives in mind. They have some idea of how to *fix* the slum, so they will go looking for individuals and families to help them accomplish this mission.

Far too often these plans crash and burn when funds dry

up, hope gives out, or the unrelenting grind of poverty becomes too overwhelming for the idealistic visitors. Unbeknownst to these well-intentioned foreigners, these failed initiatives often leave a trail of broken relationships, mistrust, and bitterness among the residents they were trying to help. After years of witnessing this phenomenon, none of Pastor Fred's congregants wanted to be the first ones I'd spring *my* agenda on.

An alley between two mud-walled houses in Kibera

Except the thing was, I *had* no agenda. I wasn't there to fix the slum. I wasn't there to start some new non-profit. I was simply there to learn at the feet of Pastor Fred, experience everyday life in the slum, and see how I could use my connections and influence to support the work of Tumaini Church.

During those two weeks of silence for *me*, Pastor Fred was being bombarded with questions from the congregation.

"What does he want?"

"Do you have to cook him special food?"

"Why is this crazy mzungu living here?"

Slowly but surely, Pastor Fred explained to them that I really *did* just want to learn, and that I hadn't come to take anything from the community. He also explained that I ate sukuma wiki and ugali with my hands, just like them. I didn't need special meals.

He must have convinced them, because about halfway through my time in Kibera, people started opening their homes. In fact, I started getting one invitation after another. Before long, a torrent of invites started flowing in and my social calendar was completely booked up. I was loafin' it multiple times per week. Apparently, once the ice had been broken, a new fear had taken the place of the old one: nobody wanted to be the only family I *didn't* visit during my stay in Kibera!

Thankfully, in the end I had earned the trust of the Tumaini Church community with my open-handed, agenda-free approach. I left that experience far more aware of how easily unintended consequences can wreak havoc in the communities we are trying to help. But I also discovered the absolute joy and privilege that can be found by truly submitting to local leaders and letting God shine through *them*.

Looking back, I am so grateful for what I learned. Yes, eating so much white bread may have been unhealthy, and I may have unintentionally developed a crippling addiction to caffeine, but now I have friends in Kibera who consider me one of their own, and I wouldn't trade that for the world.

9

Downtown

Hope beats guilt every time.

It was like driving through a war zone. Massive armored cars rumbled down the street, mounted with heavy machine guns. Rows of American troops in combat fatigues stood on the side of the road armed with assault rifles. Giant C-130 cargo planes took off and landed at the airport while dual-engined Osprey helicopters unloaded their cargo. As our motorcycle wound its way through the chaos, I could do little but take it all in with wide eyes. It felt a bit like the end of the world.

But this wasn't war. This wasn't combat. This was a humanitarian rescue mission. I was driving into Port-au-Prince, Haiti, just two weeks after an earthquake brought the island nation to its knees.

Sandwiched between my interpreter and the driver, I sat on the middle seat of our motorcycle and tried to keep my balance. Zipping around armored troop transports without a helmet on, I should have been concerned with my safety.

Instead, it was all I could do just to process the images I was seeing. Three and four story buildings now stood as heaps of rubble spilling onto the street. Many of them, I knew, still had dead bodies inside.

After passing a seemingly endless collection of ramshackle tent camps in every available open space, we reached our destination, downtown Port-au-Prince. My interpreter, John, stepped off the back of the motorcycle, and I did the same. He spoke to the motorcycle driver in Creole, arranging our return journey a few hours later.

As the motorcycle drove off, John and I took a look around.

"Where do you want to go?" he asked.

"Uh, I don't know," I said, shakily. I had no discernible skills to offer other than my ability to take photos and tell stories, and the *last* thing I wanted to do was whip out my camera. I already felt a bit like a voyeur just for being there. "Maybe we could go see the White House?"

The White House was Haiti's version of *the* White House in Washington D.C. As the country's presidential palace, it had been a proud symbol of national freedom and democracy to Haitians, but now stood shattered and collapsed. The crooked domes and broken pillars had become something of an iconic symbol of the earthquake's horror. It was as good a place to start as any, I supposed.

We began heading down a main street, forced by piles of rubble to weave back and forth as we walked. I couldn't believe what I was seeing. Cars lay crushed under cement blocks. Twisted strands of rebar sprouted out of broken walls. Every now and then I saw a handful of people using shovels to pick through the wreckage, but most of the collapsed buildings were completely untouched. In our entire trip downtown, I saw *one* industrial excavator working to clear out a damaged property. One.

After walking for a few minutes past mind-numbing destruction, we arrived at Haiti's White House. I took in a sharp breath at what I saw. It wasn't the building itself that caused me such surprise. It was the shockingly crowded tent camp that had sprung up in the park across the street.

This was an image I hadn't expected downtown. I had assumed Port-au-Prince would be like a ghost town. Instead, it was *teeming* with people. Tent after tent, crammed into every available space. The collapsed presidential palace was iconic, but now there were hundreds, if not thousands, of people for whom this scene was their home.

The tent camp in front of Haiti's shattered White House

As we walked through this tent camp, I struggled to understand all the jarring images I was seeing. A man pushed a cart full of soft drinks, hoping to make a bit of money to buy food. A woman crossed the street, balancing on her head a large bag of rice with an American flag printed on it. An elderly man sat at the entrance to a small tent, staring off into space. Life continued to go on for the people of Haiti, but their everyday existence had fundamentally changed.

As we rounded a street corner, I saw an image I don't think I will ever forget. There, in the middle of what was once a public park fountain, was a topless woman bathing herself and her two naked toddlers. Hundreds of people walked by - pedestrians, police officers, street vendors... This woman had surrendered all sense of privacy and dignity out of sheer necessity, and nobody batted an eye. The image was seared into my brain.

At that point, I felt a sense of numb helplessness crawling over me. The rest of our time downtown was a bit of a blur. At some point, our motorcycle driver picked us up and took us back to Pastor Pierre's house on the edge of town.

That night, I took a folding chair up on the roof, looked out over the city and thought about people dead under the rubble, children without parents, and families searching for food. Within moments I was weeping - just bawling my eyes out in great heaving sobs. I didn't have the capacity to understand how so much horrific desperation was even possible. Worse, I didn't know where the *hope* was in all of it.

This was a big problem. One of the absolute foundations of World Next Door was that we always ended our articles with hope. Ask any of our past summer interns, and they'll tell you I was a broken record about it. "You *always* end with hope."

I don't believe guilt is an effective motivator for life-long change. Sure, you may be able to guilt people into writing a check, but it takes something far more powerful to change that person's *lifestyle*. It takes visions of God's kingdom at work. It takes dreams of a transformed world. It takes *hope*.

Except, sitting on Pastor Pierre's roof that night, thinking back over the scenes of desolation I had witnessed just a few hours before, I couldn't find it. I had to write an article about what I had seen that day. My job was to tell stories of God's kingdom healing the brokenness of the world. That was my responsibility, but I couldn't think of a single thing to say.

After a lot of wrestling, I finally realized where *some* hope could be found. It wasn't big. It wasn't grandiose. It wasn't even guaranteed to compel my readers to take action. But it was true.

The hope I found was this: I would *never* be the same after my day downtown. *My* perspective on the world had been changed, and I would *always* carry these images with me. I made the decision that night to weave the realities of Haiti into the fabric of my life and to become an advocate for the nation, especially when the eyes of the world turned away, as they inevitably would.

If I did, I realized, then as the rebuilding of the nation continued, I would be able to share in the joys of a God who loves to restore. When hope and life finally sprang up among the wreckage, I would be able to participate in the celebration. God would not forget the people of Haiti, and from that moment on, neither would I.

10

Father

I think I gain 15 pounds every time I visit.

Following Esperandieu Pierre through the village of Chambrun was exhausting. We were just popping in to say hello to a few families, but I had trouble keeping up. Pierre, who had been serving in that community for many years, was something of a local celebrity. He seemed to know the names of every single person and of course they all knew him.

Rounding the corner of a mud hut, I found Esperandieu bantering with two elderly ladies. He had them giggling like schoolgirls before throwing his arms around their shoulders for a photo. Our whirlwind tour continued. Greetings, shouted jokes, laughter… it was a community event. Before long, a band of children had formed an entourage around Pastor Pierre. He picked a little girl up in his arms and started marching away with his "prisoner." The other kids burst into laughter and cheers, and chased after them to "rescue" their friend, who was giggling helplessly in Esperandieu's arms.

Out of nowhere, I was struck with an image of Jesus and

his disciples. I pictured Jesus walking through a village just like Esperandieu, bringing joy and life to the people he met, goofing off with kids, and leaving his disciples sweaty and frustrated behind him. I imagined them shaking their heads, wondering why Jesus wouldn't just focus on all the "important" things they had to do.

Esperandieu Pierre in the village of Chambrun

It's such a different image than the standard one I picked up as a child - the stoic, mystical Jesus, telling inscrutable parables while staring fixedly into oblivion. This was an image of Jesus *alive*. Vibrant. It was beautiful. It became a go-to reference point for me as I sought to understand the person and character of my savior.

Over the next few years, I experienced several more of these "bookmark" moments - ordinary Christ-followers displaying the *extraordinary* characteristics of the triune God. Meditating on these images has become a significant part of my own faith journey, and has given new meaning to the name *Emmanuel*, God with us. One, in particular, has put its roots deep into my heart, because it has helped me understand the fatherhood of God in a way I never quite grasped before.

It happened while I was stuffing my face in Ukraine.

The first time I visited Zhytomyr, I had a chance to live with an incredible man named Peter Levchenko. "Pastor Peter," as everyone called him, was larger than life. Boisterous, jolly, and outgoing, he was always ready with a welcoming smile and bear hug whenever new visitors came to town. Pastor Peter only knew a handful of English phrases, but he loved saying them as much as possible: "Praise God! Thank you very much." His wife, Vera, was the quintessential babushka, head scarf and all. The two of them made quite a pair.

Along with his wonderful kindness and hospitality, Pastor Peter was a dedicated church planter. He was pretty much single handedly responsible for starting thriving churches across an entire region of rural Ukraine. The man was a legend. But of all the things people loved about Pastor Peter, the epic dinner parties he hosted stood head and shoulders above the rest.

Pastor Peter was like a grandfather to everyone he met.

Pastor Peter and Vera took great delight in feeding guests, so every time a team came through town to work with Mission to Ukraine, we would cram into their tiny dining room, sit shoulder to shoulder, and eat until we thought we'd explode.

Every meal started with no less than six different appetizers. Then came the soups (plural), the bread, the vegetables, the potatoes, the meat, more bread, some fruit, *more* meat, and then at *least* four different desserts. By the end of the meal, serving dishes would be stacked on top of each other three or four high, and we would all be groaning in pain.

During one of these incredible meals, we were chowing down like normal, but I found myself observing Peter and Vera more carefully than usual. Vera, of course, was in and out of the kitchen like a babushka tornado, but Peter had taken a break to watch everyone enjoying themselves. We were all laughing and telling stories and having a *ball*, and it was clear this made Pastor Peter incredibly happy. He stood in the corner of the room with his arms crossed and a huge, satisfied grin on his face.

Yet again, I was unexpectedly struck with an image, this time of God the father. I started to grasp what it actually means for a father to take great delight in giving his children good things. Sure, Pastor Peter was not actually our biological *dad*, but in that space, we *were* a part of his family. In the same way, I realized, we are all adopted children of God. When we take joy in the good things of this earth, the Father is sincerely pleased. The image of Peter smiling in the corner put flesh on that concept for me. Now, when I want to think about the fatherhood of God, I have a bookmark I can turn to - a concrete image that reveals the character of the Creator.

Ultimately, these images are incomplete. No human person can fully capture the depth and grandeur and beauty of the Father, Son, and Holy Spirit. But I am constantly on the lookout for more. I want to know my savior, and seeing his personality lived out through his followers is a great place to start.

11

White Cloth

I wish I could have been at the wedding.

Baby Rachel and I stared at each other. It was the first time we had met, and she was not quite sure how she felt about me. With chubby cheeks and wide, brown eyes, she stared at me as if trying to decide if I was friend or foe. Undeterred by her skepticism, I made a funny face. That did the trick. The baby's face lit up in a bright smile. I couldn't help but smile back.

We were sitting in the shade of a large mango tree in the courtyard of a Cambodian house on the edge of the city. The couple I had come to meet (the baby's parents) had just told me the story of how they met, and it filled my heart with unspeakable joy. This baby, I realized, represented something far deeper than just the beauty and innocence of new life.

This baby represented redemption.

—

The story of this beautiful family started at a place called Rapha House, a safe-house for girls rescued from sex trafficking, which I had the privilege to visit during my stay in

Cambodia in 2010.

At the time I visited, Rapha House was home to 104 formerly trafficked girls. Rescued by organizations like International Justice Mission, the girls had been given a safe place to live while they picked up the pieces of their broken lives.

Director S., the man in charge of day-to-day operations at the safe house, took time out of his schedule to show me around. We walked through the gate and into the main building. On the balcony staring down at us was a row of smiling, seemingly carefree girls. They waved and shouted greetings. I smiled and waved back, a bit caught off guard by how young some of them looked.

Inside the building were many other girls. Some were practicing on sewing machines, others were studying English. When they saw me, they all shouted out "Hello!" and "How are you today?"

Frankly, it was a rather happy place. I was struck by how peaceful it all felt. It wasn't until I began interviewing Director S. in his office that I remembered what brought these girls to Rapha House in the first place.

As he explained to me what many of the girls have been through in their lives, my smile quickly faded away.

———

Most of the sex trafficking I wrote about during my time in Cambodia was small-scale; families selling their daughters to local brothels for money. It's the kind of sex trafficking people don't tend to think about, but it's a reality for far too many girls around the world. That said, there is another kind of trafficking in Cambodia that plagues impoverished girls, and it *does* tend to align with what we imagine: organized, international crime.

Although some of the girls at Rapha House had been saved from local brothels, many fell into this second category. As we began the interview, Director S. explained their background.

Some of these girls were tricked by the promise of a good job in a neighboring country. They piled into trucks headed for

Bangkok or Kuala Lumpur or Hanoi, excited about the prospect of steady income, only to find themselves imprisoned in a foreign brothel with no way to get back home. A few of the other girls decided to be prostitutes willingly to help provide for their families, but had no idea just how horrific and scarring the experience would be.

Whatever their reason, the girls at Rapha House had all at some point been trafficked for sex.

When I heard this, I asked Director S., "Why do the girls stay in the brothels? Why don't they just run away?"

The answers were very hard to hear.

First of all, he explained, these girls are often lost in cities far from home. They don't speak the language, they don't know their way around, and they are told that if they go to the police they will be thrown in jail for prostitution. In other words, they are dreadfully afraid to leave.

I was horrified to learn what faces many girls in Cambodia.

For many who *do* go to the police, the results are not much better. Because the sex trafficking industry is so lucrative, many police are on the payroll of local brothels. Rather than rescuing suffering girls, the police take them right back to their pimps, often after raping and beating them in the police station to "teach the girls a lesson."

I started feeling sick to my stomach. Trying to wrap my head around what he was telling me, I asked Director S., "So that's why Rapha House has barbed wire and 24 hour security? To keep out the people who might want to steal back these girls?"

"Partly," he said. "But it's not just to keep the bad people out. It's also to keep the new girls in."

I didn't understand what he meant. The high walls and armed guards were there to keep the girls *in*?!? Why would they ever want to leave?

Director S. started explaining how absolutely brainwashed many of these girls had become. Sometimes the manipulation starts with simple violence. Girls are beaten if they try to escape. They're beaten if they refuse to have sex with a customer. They're beaten if they don't act like they're enjoying it.

After a couple of years, trafficked girls often become willing pawns in the cycle of abuse. Before too long they find *themselves* doing the beating when new girls are brought in. They find *themselves* standing on the streets late at night, calling out seductively to potential customers, eager to avoid another split lip or black eye.

Many trafficked girls are given drugs like heroin by their pimps and madams to induce compliance and to create hopeless addictions. Even if they are able to escape, they often come running back when their cravings become too much to handle.

That's why Rapha House built the walls. Far too often, scared, addicted, and hopeless girls try to escape so they can go back to the brothels from which they were rescued.

As we came to the end of our conversation, my heart was a swirl of emotion. I was filled with fury, hopelessness, anger, frustration, and pain. I couldn't wrap my mind around the sheer evil and horror of what these girls had been through.

Director S. led me out of his office to continue the tour. Once more, I saw all the beautiful, smiling girls. Once more, I did my best to smile back. But I couldn't shake the knowledge of what they had experienced.

For some reason I felt compelled to ask one more follow-up question.

"Director S., how old is the youngest girl in your program?"

"Our youngest girl is six," he replied.

My heart shattered into a million tiny pieces on the floor.

———

I was moments away from drifting into hopelessness. Thankfully, Director S. began showing me how Rapha House worked to restore and rehabilitate these girls. What I learned gave me a glimmer of hope in the midst of the darkness.

Rapha House had a fully trained staff of psychologists and counselors to help the girls work through the trauma they had experienced. They had house parents and teachers that loved on the girls daily. They had a trusted security team to keep the girls safe.

Throughout their stay, the girls were trained in sewing, hairdressing, and English. Every year, 10 girls "graduated" and moved into a halfway house. Eventually, they were reintegrated back into society, armed with a whole new set of professional skills.

Next door to Rapha House was a church. Every Sunday, the girls were invited to join people from the surrounding community for worship. Not all attended, but many did. Quite a few of the girls had become Christ-followers and had experienced tremendous spiritual and emotional healing in the process.

If there was any place in the world that was right for these broken lives, I realized, it was Rapha House.

And yet, as we walked around the compound, I couldn't help but think about the Cambodian proverb I had heard a couple of days before. It went like this: "Men are like gold. Women are like white cloth."

Its meaning is pretty simple. If gold gets dirty, you can just wipe it off. It looks brand new. If white cloth gets dirty, it can never be perfectly clean again. You can wash it as much as you want, but it will never be as pure as it once was. The consequences of this way of thinking are pretty clear. Cambodian men don't want to marry "soiled" girls.

All the girls I met at Rapha House had been robbed of their innocence. Their hopes for the future, for getting married and having a family, were shattered forever. Even with phenomenal rehabilitation programs, their lives would never be the same, would they?

———

To answer that question, I sought out two people I had heard about before my visit. From what I understood, they were house parents for some recent graduates of Rapha House. I asked Director S. if we could visit them to hear their story. He agreed.

We left the safe house compound and walked down the street to a nearby home. There, this couple lived with six girls who had finished the Rapha House program but had no families to go back to.

The girls lived fairly normal lives. They rode bikes to school each day, they ate meals with their house parents and "sisters," and helped out with household chores. Their surrogate mom and dad did their best to give the girls a safe and loving home. In fact, for most of the girls living there, this was the first time they had ever lived with a truly safe family.

As we entered the gate to the property, I was excited to meet the house parents. We sat down in their shady courtyard and they told me how they met.

The house father, we'll call him Touyou, used to be part of the security team at Rapha House. He worked shifts at the gate, patrolled the yard and kept a watchful eye on new visitors. Every Sunday, 17-year-old Touyou would play the keyboard at church.

Some of the girls from the Rapha House program, rescued from sex trafficking and slowly healing from years of terrible pain, would join Touyou on stage to perform graceful dances as part of the worship service. One of those girls, also 17 years old, was Sitaa.

It didn't take long for Touyou to notice Sitaa (she really is quite stunning!). Her dancing was so graceful that Touyou was immediately captivated.

Every week he would play the keyboard and every week she would dance. After a few months of this, Touyou fell madly in love with Sitaa. And as it turned out, the feeling was mutual.

But what to do? The rules of Rapha House were quite clear. There was no way a security guard could court one of the girls in the program. The only option was to wait.

So, wait they did. For five years.

By the time Sitaa was ready to graduate from the program, everybody knew how much she and Touyou loved each other. And everybody approved of the match. Touyou was a fine, upstanding young man and Sitaa was a gracious and tender young woman.

So, at 22 years of age, Sitaa and Touyou were married. It was a huge celebration. There was music, dancing, and food. It was a party to remember.

All of the girls from Rapha House attended, and it was a hugely significant moment for them. Through Sitaa's example they saw that their lives were not over. That they were still worthy of love.

Sitaa, walking down the aisle in a beautiful flowing gown, encapsulated the concept of new life. Touyou, standing there nervous but proud, captured the concept of grace.

Girls may be white cloth, as the proverb goes, and they can get dirty. But on the day that Touyou married Sitaa, the Rapha House girls saw that there is a God of love who can wash them white as snow.

After the wedding, Touyou and Sitaa moved into a new home and became the house parents they still were when I visited. For years they had demonstrated the concept of grace to their "daughters" through simple acts of love and compassion.

Sitaa, once desperate and broken in a brothel far from home, was now a living and breathing demonstration of hope. Touyou, overcoming the prejudices his culture had imposed, daily demonstrated that there *were* good men in the world.

Oh, and there is something else. Nine months before I met them, Touyou and Sitaa brought into this world a little bundle of life. They gave birth to a baby girl. As they told me their story in the fading afternoon light, little baby Rachel stood bouncing on her mother's lap. Locking eyes with this precious little girl, it was all I could do not to just burst into tears.

In every way I could think of, this baby was a symbol of the kingdom of God. Redemption, grace, hope, and love were wrapped up in this little one. Baby Rachel was there because of Rapha House. She was there because of grace. She was there because her mother found a new identity in Christ. And she was there because her father chose to love selflessly.

That wiggly, giggly bundle of joy was proof that in this dark world the kingdom of God is at work and nothing, not even the depths of human depravity, can stand in its way. Hope is on the move.

———

As I left Rapha House that day, I struggled under the heavy weight of awareness I had taken on. Seeing a whole community of girls victimized by an evil injustice was almost too much to process emotionally.

But as we drove away from the compound, I held on to a deep inner hope by plastering a single image all over the walls of my heart: little baby Rachel and her beautiful, care-free smile.

12

Spare Change

Best hot dog I've ever had

I was homeless when I met Anthony Bourdain.

We were boarding the Staten Island ferry in New York City. He was surrounded by his film crew. I was alone. Although my clothes were grungy, my hair was a mess, and my breath stank from days without brushing, I couldn't help but introduce myself. I waited for a moment when his crew was distracted, walked up, and greeted him.

"Mr. Bourdain, my dad and I really love your show," I said, smiling.

He gave a distracted half-smile back, said, "Oh, thanks," then walked off to start filming. I filed onto the ferry with the rest of the crowd, then rode it back and forth for an hour, wondering when (or if) I'd be able to find food that day.

Bourdain, a world-traveling chef and TV host, was something of an inspiration for me as I started World Next Door. His love of other cultures and willingness to try new things had always impressed me, especially being the terrified, picky-eating homebody I was for most of my life. So it was the essence of irony that I met him while on "assignment" for World Next Door.

It was the spring of 2010. I was writing about the work of New York City Relief, a ministry that drives a modified soup truck, the "Relief Bus," to the different boroughs of the city each day to bring food, love, and connections to struggling people. To help me understand the issue of homelessness, I felt it was necessary to experience homelessness myself, at least for a while. So, with the blessing of the NYCR staff, I set off to spend four days and three nights living alone on the streets. My only assets were a book to read, a 7 day unlimited metro card, my old cell phone, my journal, a Bible, 25 cents, and the clothes on my back. To say the experience was eye-opening would be an understatement. Put simply, I'll never look at homelessness the same way again.

On my first night in the city I slept deep in the tunnels of Penn Station, tossing and turning on the cold floor with my backpack as a pillow. Scared and uncertain about what might happen to me, I jolted awake at each sound I heard. When the police woke me up at 4am to clear the building for incoming commuters, I discovered that hundreds of other people had also taken shelter in the station in the night. Almost every nook and cranny was occupied by someone without a home. It was a fascinating glimpse into an unseen world that was completely gone come dawn.

For my second and third evenings, I checked into a homeless shelter, sleeping on the top bunk in a room full of snoring men. As we shuffled between the sleeping area and dining hall, I had a chance to chat with a few of the other residents. To my surprise, many of these men had jobs and really high standards for cleanliness and personal grooming. It's embarrassing to admit, but this wasn't something I usually associated with homeless people.

Throughout this four-day episode on the streets I felt the loneliness of being grungy and dirty in a city full of beautiful people, I experienced the humility of standing in line at a soup kitchen while fancy cars drove by, and I felt the helplessness of being broke in a place where *everything* costs money. But of all the things I learned and experienced during my short stint on the streets, there was one lesson that hit me far deeper the rest. It's a memory that will be with me for the rest of my life. This life-changing experience was panhandling.

During my first day, I spent most of the afternoon simply trying to work up the courage to start asking for money. Every time I got close to starting, my subconscious would start yelling at me. *What will people think of me? Will they be upset? What if I get arrested or something?* Unrealistic fears began to seep in to my heart. But as dusk approached, my stomach started to growl. It was then I realized the truth of my situation. As I said above, I had no money with me at all, and no "bail-out" option like a credit card to fall back on. If I didn't start panhandling, I wouldn't eat dinner. Simple as that.

So, abandoning any sense of independence or self-sufficiency, I squatted down next to a wall, held out my hands and begged.

"Can you spare a dollar, sir? Ma'am, can I have a quarter?"

As you might imagine, most people walked right by. A few genuinely didn't notice me, but most deliberately avoided eye contact. Every now and then, someone would look down at me and quickly look away, as if I could somehow trap them with my mind. One lady gave me a dollar, but otherwise I was coming up empty. After 10 or 15 minutes, being ignored started to get to me. I switched spots and tried again. Same situation. The vast majority of people simply walked right by.

From the moment I decided to try this experience, I knew it would happen. I knew I would be treated as worthless. But having it actually happen time and time again brought the reality of it all straight to my heart. *I had no idea how awful this would be,* I thought. Being ignored is a terrible, terrible feeling. I panhandled for probably a grand total of 45 minutes and already I was starting to feel less than human. I wanted to stand up and shout, "Hey! At least acknowledge me as a person!"

But despite my frustration, there were a few bright spots through it all. Occasionally, someone would look me in the eyes, reach into their pockets and genuinely say, "I'm sorry. I wish I could help you", before moving on. You'd think that I would have been annoyed by that, but I wasn't. In fact, simply being acknowledged at all was extraordinarily uplifting. I couldn't help but smile at them, even though my pockets were still empty.

Over the course of my time panhandling, I ended up making about $8.50 (due in large part to a $5 bill a man gave me in a subway stairwell). Because I only needed enough money to buy dinner and breakfast, I quit. I was feeling guilty enough taking other people's money. I walked out of the subway station and towards a hotdog stand. $2 for a hotdog with everything on it. It wasn't going to get much cheaper than that in Manhattan.

As I ate, tears welled up in my eyes. I was overwhelmed with emotions. In a short amount of time, I had felt the bitterness of being ignored, the gratitude of simple eye contact, and the humility that comes from being fully dependent on the good will of another.

Looking back, I know I was never in a place of true desperation. I can never claim to fully understand what it's like having no choice but to live on the streets. But my four days homeless in Manhattan changed my life. The experience caused me to rethink old assumptions, open my eyes to the invisible suffering happening around me, and forever alter the way I treat panhandlers I meet. Even if I can't give them any money, I will *always* try to offer them the gift of dignity.

———

At the end of my time on the streets, I took the subway out to meet the Relief Bus in the Bronx. As I walked up to the big, white bus, I had a whole new appreciation for their approach to ministry. Their philosophy is to look past outward appearances and see the children of God underneath the dirty clothing, addictions, and despair. Day after day, lonely and downtrodden people come to eat soup from The Relief Bus.

But more than that, they come to feel like people again. They come for the prayer, the encouragement, and the smiles.

And the NYCR staff and volunteers are more than willing to oblige them. Their actions are steeped in the life and teachings of Jesus. They are living out the kingdom of God in one of the most basic and beautiful of ways: giving life and dignity to those that have none.

Each day before heading off to the city, everybody on The Relief Bus gathers around and chants a simple phrase (shouting the second half):

"These things we do... SO THAT OTHERS MAY LIVE!!!"

And after four lonely days on the streets of Manhattan, when I walked up to the Relief Bus to get my own cup of soup, the smiles, handshakes and love *I* received did something remarkable. They made me feel *alive.*

13

Culinary Empathy

I still don't know what the stringy things were.

One day in Cambodia I found myself in an intense staring contest with a quail. It was dead, of course. And fried. And part of my lunch. But that didn't change the fact that its vacant eyes were staring up at me, unblinking: a steady reminder that even in death the bird had a deep and abiding contempt for my species.

I imagined the quail's life. I though of him running majestically across the jungle floor, dreaming big dreams as he headed off to quail college. High-fiving his new dorm buddies, he had no idea he was about to be caught, killed, and deep fried for my mid-day meal. While I was deep in thought contemplating my own role in the demise of this majestic creature, someone suggested I take a bite. Because I try to always say "yes" to new experiences, I picked up a piece with the head still attached, ripped off a bit of meat from the neck and chewed.

It tasted like chicken. It felt like murder.

I used to be a super-picky eater. Ten years ago I couldn't eat anything with a bone still on it, much less a *face*. Brussels sprouts made me nauseous. Seafood made me gag. Let's just say I didn't have a very adventurous palate. If a restaurant served Italian food, I ordered pizza. If it served American food, I ordered a hamburger. End of story.

Which begs the question. How in the world was I able to eat deep fried quail neck in Cambodia without barfing all over the wall? How did I go from squeamish at the sight of shrimp to smiling as I gulped down a spicy Mekong river snail? How could I swallow fried tarantula, goat brains, duck embryo, goat intestines, deep fried whole frogs, goat heart, cow tongue, the *rest* of the goat, durian fruit, and chicken gizzards without curling up into a ball and crying myself to sleep?

Honestly, I didn't know the answer for a while. It took me several years to figure this out, but eventually the pieces fell into place. Essentially, it comes down to this: because I am not naturally adventurous or blessed with an iron stomach, I've had to draw on a *different* skill to get me through these culinary challenges. Something that isn't usually associated with cuisine. That skill? Empathy.

You see, I'm usually a pretty empathetic person. I am aware of the feelings of others, able to put myself in their shoes and see the world from their perspective. Frankly, it's one of the reasons I started World Next Door in the first place. One day not too long ago, as I was debriefing my most recent culinary exploits with my parents, I put two and two together and realized how empathy plays a role in my eating.

"Whenever I have to eat something weird," I told them, "I just remind myself that people *here* eat this. That this is normal to them." Looking at the weird food from their perspective, suddenly it doesn't seem quite so revolting.

This, for example, is how I was able to take my first few bites of giant, wriggly oysters on Penelakut Island in British Columbia. I was embedded with an organization working on a First Nations (a.k.a. "Native American") reservation. One afternoon, Tim, one of the ministry's leaders, and I went out with one of the local elders to collect huge oysters from the beach. We filled buckets full of barnacled oyster shells, built up a fire, then cooked the oysters in their own shells. Even though I still had a hard time enjoying the taste of seafood, I managed to get the oysters down with a smile on my face. All I had to do was remember how much the locals love them and suddenly they weren't so bad.

Surprisingly, Durian fruit was one of the worst things I ever tried. It tasted 90% delicious and 10% like a rotting cat carcass.

With practice, this "culinary empathy" has become a routine part of my travels. The coolest thing about all of this, however, is that it has begun to expand. Now it is more than simply saying "yes" when weird foods are put in front of me. To my own surprise, I've begun to try new things *voluntarily*.

The first time I was in Cambodia I took a five-hour bus ride from Phnom Penh to Battambang. At about 10am, the bus stopped at a rest area for a few minutes. Being the only white guy around, and not knowing what bus-stop etiquette was in those parts, I had to watch what everyone else was doing and simply follow along.

"Okay, looks like everyone is walking over to the toilets…

Yep, I can handle that. Flushing the urinal with a ladle from a nearby basin? Okay… And now everybody is walking over and buying noodles and some sort of soup. Hmm, well I *am* hungry…"

As I walked up to buy some noodles, my more practical, comfort-loving self began to protest. "Uh oh. Those veggies were washed with unclean water. She just touched those noodles with her bare hands! What exactly are those round, stringy things floating in the soup?"

I was about to walk away when my culinary empathy kicked in. I looked around, saw a ton of other people eating noodles and realized, "If they are all eating them, how bad can they be?" I paid for the noodles, took my bowl to a nearby table and started chowing down with a pair of chopsticks. Maybe I shouldn't have been surprised, but they were delicious.

After many years of practice, my culinary empathy has led me to eat some pretty crazy stuff. I don't always enjoy the things I put in my mouth - tarantula tasted like arachnid-flavored cooking oil with just a *hint* of leg hair, and durian fruit made me gag - but at least I can eat it all with a smile!

14

The Wall

---

*Why anybody would construct flooring
out of eggshells is beyond me.*

I got chills when I first saw the wall.

Looking up, all I could see was concrete and metal. The height of a three story building, the impassable barrier was topped with a row of barbed wire. Looking to my right and left, the barrier stretched off as far as I could see in both directions. In the distance, it wound up and down over hillsides like the Great Wall of China.

A constant stream of murals, spray-painted slogans, artwork and graffiti covered the wall, interrupted only by guard towers and the occasional reinforced steel doorway.

The wall I was looking at was the West Bank Separation Barrier. When it is completed, the wall will be 470 miles long and will separate Israel almost completely from the West Bank. The barrier (or "security fence" or "segregation wall" depending on who you are talking to), is being built by the

Israeli government to stem the tide of suicide bombings by terrorists coming from across the border.

The wall prevents anyone in the West Bank without a permit from crossing into Israel. And although it has reportedly reduced terrorism significantly since its construction, the wall is a source of a lot of tension and disagreement both locally and internationally.

A guard tower on the West Bank Separation Barrier

Almost immediately after coming to the Holy Land, I heard Palestinians share how humiliating and dehumanizing the wall can be. I heard Israelis talk about the horrific insecurities of life before the fence. When talking about the issue of the wall, just about everyone felt victimized in some way. In a sense, the wall is a symbol. It represents much of the conflict between Israelis and Palestinians and strongly highlights just how complicated the situation can be.

———

For about four weeks in the spring of 2011 I lived in an apartment in Bethlehem (yes, *that* Bethlehem). Because it's located in the West Bank, I had to go through the security barrier every day to make my way to the office of my host ministry, Musalaha, in Jerusalem.

During one of these trips through the wall, the checkpoint was especially packed with people. It was a Friday morning, so crowds of Palestinian Muslims were heading into Jerusalem to worship at the Al-Aqsa mosque, the third holiest site in Islam. I stood in line behind an elderly man with a long beard and a brilliant white keffiyeh on his head.

At first everyone was in a good mood. Men shook hands with old friends. Women chatted together. But as the monotonous waiting dragged on, peoples' patience started wearing thin.

The line crawled forward. Every now and then, someone from the back of the line would walk to the front and try sneakily cutting in line. Most times this would cause a chorus of angry shouts and arguments. It was hot. It was crowded. By the time I finally reached the metal detector and x-ray machine, everyone around me was in a pretty sour mood. I was no exception.

The checkpoint metal detector was chaotic. People went back and forth to get plastic bins, older folks dropped coins, soldiers behind bullet proof glass gave orders. On this day I managed to get through relatively quickly, which is more than can be said for some of the people next to me in line.

Through another turnstile, I entered the document check area. Since the Second Intifada, a Palestinian uprising in 2000 that led to much violence on both sides, Palestinians have been required to have permits if they want to enter Israel from the West Bank.

Although I could generally breeze through with my American passport, most Palestinians had to show their permits and submit to a fingerprint scan. Israeli guards stood around holding assault rifles. I watched as one frustrated Israeli soldier argued with a Palestinian man about whether his permit was valid.

Finally, an hour and a half after entering, I made it out of the checkpoint, down a concrete ramp and onto a waiting bus headed for Jerusalem.

I found a seat and was just about to pop in my headphones

and listen to my favorite podcast when a woman in her late sixties sat next to me. She had a large white bandage over her left eye and looked completely frazzled after getting through the checkpoint.

I put my headphones down and gave her a quick smile. She gave a half-hearted smile back, but then let out a sigh and put her hand to her head.

"Wow. It was pretty crowded today, huh?" I asked.

"It is terrible. Terrible!" she said. "They treat us like animals." She took her entry permit and identification card out of her purse and handed them to me. "Look at that. Like animals."

She went on to explain that she is a Catholic Palestinian who had recently had eye surgery and needed to return to a hospital in Jerusalem for more treatment.

Because of her physical condition, she wasn't able to lean down without help. However, in the checkpoint an Israeli guard made her lean over to take off her shoes. She had tears in her eyes as she told me how humiliating it was.

"I am an old woman! Who am I going to kill?"

Just then the bus started to roll. She slowly shook her head and said, "Someday soon this will all be gone. Someday soon the king will come." Then she rocked gently back and forth and repeated, "He will be king. He will be king. He will be king."

I murmured a quiet agreement, a bit stunned to hear hope for the kingdom of God expressed in such a simple, tangible way.

After a few moments, she grew quiet. I smiled and began asking about her family. We chatted for a few minutes about her home, but eventually the conversation turned back to the security wall.

"Nobody knows what happens here," she said. "It's very painful."

"That's actually why I'm here," I told her. "I'm a writer. I'm trying to write about what life is really like here so that people back home can understand."

Suddenly she got very serious. She turned, stared straight into my eyes and pointed her finger at me.

"Write this," she said. "Write this."

After saying this, she started digging through her purse. She pulled out a small devotional bracelet (cheap wooden beads with pictures of the saints on them) and handed it to me. She didn't explain why.

I thanked her and looked up. Unfortunately, my stop was next. I apologized that we couldn't talk more and said a quick goodbye. Then I stood, walked down the aisle and stepped off the bus. As I walked down the street towards the Musalaha office, her words echoed in my head.

"Write this."

———

As my trip wore on, I began thinking of the security barrier less as a physical boundary and more as a symbol of something deeper. It represented, for me at least, the metaphorical walls we all choose to build in our hearts. Walls of hatred, racism, and dehumanization divide us, one from another. As an outsider looking in at the Israeli/Palestinian conflict, I could see the effects of these walls lived out before my eyes.

For example, in my conversations with locals I had to walk on eggshells all the time. I was constantly putting my foot in my mouth. Once I referred to the region as "Israel," and was quickly scolded by a Palestinian teenager.

"What, you think Israel *owns* this land? You think they have a right to occupy our homes?"

"Uh…" I replied, unsure of how to respond.

Another time, I mentioned my interest in the topic of "social justice" and had my head nearly bitten off by an Israeli college student.

"Oh, *social justice*? So you think we should just divide up everything and give free handouts to people who don't deserve it? You think we should just give our land to the Palestinians?"

Again, "Uh…"

People I met on both sides of the divide seemed intent on reducing those on the other side to broad, simple categories.

And I suppose I don't blame them. When a bomb goes off, it's easier to think of Palestinians as uncivilized, angry fanatics than as intelligent and hard-working people trying to make their way in the world. When the tanks roll in, it's simpler to see Israelis as manipulative and land-grabbing elitists than as a persecuted people looking for a home. When emotions run high, nuance and perspective tend to disappear. And so we build walls in our hearts and work hard to keep those borders secure.

However, despite the seemingly intractable divides and hostile opinions I encountered, my time in the Holy Land was not without hope. My days were spent shadowing the leaders of Musalaha, an organization dedicated to tearing down the walls that separate people. Their staff, comprised of Israeli and Palestinian Christ-followers, was tireless in their efforts to "re-humanize" each other and seek love as the ultimate source of reconciliation.

I watched as Musalaha led Israeli and Palestinian high schoolers on a "desert encounter" that revealed their shared humanity. I heard stories of hope from a Palestinian man whose family had been forcibly ejected from their homeland. I heard an Israeli who lost friends in a suicide attack talk about her love for Palestinians. It was like hearing snippets of a beautiful symphony cutting through the static on the radio. And the music was growing in strength.

And so the words of the Palestinian lady on the bus continued to echo in my heart.

"Write this."

I had a responsibility to tell the story, not just of how broken the situation was, but of how the light of the kingdom was shining through. Yes, there were walls dividing people in the Holy Land. Racial and religious and cultural and historical divides had left giant barriers in peoples' hearts. But I got to witness cracks forming in these walls.

I saw Israeli and Palestinian Christ-followers loving each other as brothers and sisters of the faith. I saw a team of dedicated kingdom agents working tirelessly to spread a message of reconciliation and peace. I saw the effects of the kingdom of God at work in our world, and left the Holy Land convinced that there is hope.

"Write this," she told me. And so I will. I will never stop telling this story I know to be true: God is working in the world. The hope of the gospel is spreading. And no barrier built by man can stand against it.

15

Peter

My beloved son, welcome home.

One of my all-time favorite stories of hope began in Zhytomyr, Ukraine, on my very first "official" trip for World Next Door.

It started at the Romaniv Disabled Boys Orphanage. As I mentioned earlier, the place was a squalid, hellish place just a few years ago. Before Mission to Ukraine started visiting, the boys living at the orphanage were treated like animals, ignored, and often abused. When I first visited, MTU had only been working at the orphanage for a year. Although they had made progress, there was still a long journey of restoration ahead of them.

Throughout my first week with MTU, I heard many people talking about a specific boy at Romaniv named Peter. The Mission to Ukraine staff went on and on about how much they loved him. Oksana Shulyuk, in particular, had a deep love for little Peter, and shared with me several times how much her heart broke for his situation.

Peter was 11 years old at the time, although he thought he was six (at Romaniv, nobody celebrated birthdays). Abandoned by his parents at a young age because of his progressive muscular dystrophy, he had spent the last six or seven years living at Romaniv. It had gradually become the only world that he knew.

Although his slowly dying muscles kept Peter confined to a wheelchair, he was mentally healthy. He could think and dream and imagine like any other boy. But the Romaniv staff had almost zero training on how to care for special needs kids. As a result, they kept him in the "severely disabled" section of the orphanage (a.k.a. the "isolation ward").

Peter at Romaniv in 2009

Instead of receiving stimulating education, conversations, and games, Peter was left alone in a corner, surrounded by "playmates" who couldn't speak, who stole his toys, and who often beat him. As you can imagine, little Peter began to develop bitterness toward God. Although he enjoyed the lively visits by the MTU staff, Peter became more and more frustrated and angry each time they had to leave. Oksana shared with me how devastating it was to hear Peter share how he didn't think God was good.

Nevertheless, Oksana and the other Mission to Ukraine staff continued to love on little Peter. Each week they showed up. Whether it was sunny or snowing or even a national holiday, they were there.

On my first visit to Romaniv in the spring of 2009, I got a chance to meet Peter in person. On my second visit, I asked Oksana if we could take him outside for an interview. She thought it was a great idea. After bundling him up and carrying him down the stairs (did I mention there were no wheelchair ramps at Romaniv?), Peter took his first breath of fresh air in months.

Moments after leaving the building, Peter looked up and happily shouted, "Sky! Sky! Sky!" We wheeled him around the property, having a little trouble asking questions through his wide-eyed excitement. "Why are those trees cut down? What are they building there? Look! A tractor... " I asked a few different questions about his life, what he liked to do, etc., doing my best to get an answer before he got distracted by something else he hadn't seen in half a year cooped up indoors. After a while, I finally asked the question Oksana had been afraid to bring up again.

"Peter, what do you think of God?"

Peter answered immediately. "He is good and he is my father."

Oksana was blown away. Stunned, she turned and told me how amazing it was to hear him say that. Her only conclusion was that God must be doing something in his heart. All week she kept talking about our interview with Peter. She just couldn't believe that his heart had softened so much.

The following week, the Mission to Ukraine team prepared a special Easter lesson for the Romaniv boys. They talked about Jesus rising from the dead and asked if any of the boys wanted to follow him. I will never forget the look on Oksana's face when the question was asked of Peter. He answered "yes." Excitedly, she asked him if he was sure and led him in a prayer. When they finished, Oksana sat back and looked around the room with a huge grin on her face. It just so happened to be her birthday, and I don't think she could have received a better present.

When it came time for us to leave, Oksana was walking around in a daze. She couldn't believe it. Peter had chosen to follow Christ! As we drove back to Zhytomyr, everyone was chattering and laughing with excitement. It was a momentous day. In that very dark place, hope had prevailed. We went about the rest of our weeks smiling from ear to ear. It was obvious God was on the move at Romaniv.

At the time, I thought that was the end of the story. I shared the beautiful tale of Peter's transformation on the World Next Door blog and left it at that. A glimmer of hope in a dark place. The end.

Little did I know that Peter's story was only just beginning.

———

Unbeknownst to me, while I was wrapping up my trip to Ukraine, there was a small group of people in suburban Indianapolis who read the Peter article and decided that they wanted to get involved somehow. They put their heads together and agreed that they would donate the money necessary for Peter to get adopted by a Ukrainian family.

They contacted Mission to Ukraine and explained their decision. The MTU staff was excited, but also sobered by the realities on the ground. They knew how hard it would be to find a family willing to adopt a child with special needs. Not only were there many cultural stigmas attached to having a child with disabilities in Ukraine, there was a major social burden as well. In a place as economically depressed as Zhytomyr, there were almost no support structures in place for people with disabilities. Finding a family willing to take on so much extra pressure and hardship would be no easy task.

Nevertheless, they agreed to start looking, hoping that God would provide a family. "We'll do our best," they said, "but we doubt any family is going to be willing."

Meanwhile, unbeknownst to *everybody*, God was working in the heart of a man named Yuri. Yuri, who happened to be my host father while I lived in Zhytomyr, had been a volunteer for

MTU on and off for a couple of years. When they started visiting Romaniv Orphanage, he had offered to drive them back and forth.

Yuri (left) with his son Taras in 2009

Initially that's all Yuri did. Drive. As time went by, however, he began helping the MTU staff as they worked with the boys. He would carry boys around, push wheelchairs, and help lead lessons and songs. Week after week, Yuri helped at Romaniv. Week after week his heart was softened.

One boy in particular touched Yuri's heart. The boy's name was Peter.

Yuri felt deep compassion for little Peter and eventually he came to a surprising conclusion. Right about the same time I was writing my article, Yuri said to himself, "I feel like God is calling me to adopt Peter, but there is no way I could ever pay for it."

As you might guess, it didn't take long for the dots to get connected. Yuri and his wife came forward, the donors followed through on their pledge, the adoption process was initiated, and on June 12, 2009, Peter left Romaniv, carried home in the arms of his new father.

I was stunned and speechless when I heard the news. God

had moved *powerfully* in just a few months, and I almost couldn't believe it. Peter was being adopted!

—

A new season of life for little Peter had begun, but a happy ending wasn't guaranteed. The original arrangement for Peter's adoption by Yuri's family was a temporary one. Peter would live with them for a year, followed by an evaluation by the state government. Even though this deadline loomed on the horizon, nothing could hide the beauty and joy of his homecoming. For a year at least, Peter would be safe.

And what a year it was! For the first time in a decade, Peter was living in a home. He had a family: a mother, a father, and siblings. Nobody was beating him. Nobody was yelling at him. Peter was being loved.

Peter's new brothers and sisters accepted him immediately. They included him in their games, watched movies with him and laughed - a lot.

Ira, Peter's new mother, gladly stepped in to provide the maternal care that Peter had never experienced. She bathed him, dressed him and loved him as if he was her own. All the while, Yuri carried Peter back and forth from his room, drove him around town, and taught him things like any good father would.

Of course, Peter still had to deal with many of the psychological ramifications of being discarded and abused for much of his childhood, and this was a constant struggle for his parents. The first time his family brought him to MTU for classes, he wept uncontrollably, thinking that he was being abandoned again. For a child as scarred as Peter, recovery would be a long road.

In time, however, his emotional wounds did begin to heal. He began to smile. To laugh. As his family held him, fed him, and played with him, Peter's life finally began to change.

But things were not idyllic forever. At the end of the year, the state government performed their evaluation. After seeing Yuri's small house and his seven children running all over the place (eight if you count Peter), they decided that Yuri only wanted to adopt Peter for the pension money he would receive for Peter's disability. Their hearts were hardened and nothing could convince them of the truth.

As part of the evaluation, these officials visited Romaniv Orphanage to see the living conditions there for themselves. However, because the orphanage staff didn't want to be embarrassed, they only allowed the state officials to see the inside of one room – a nicely furnished conference room used solely for visiting guests.

After seeing this sugar-coated image of the orphanage (and after stumbling through a lot of bureaucratic inefficiency and lost paperwork), the state officials declared that the living conditions were far better for Peter at Romaniv than at Yuri's home. Then they made a decision that absolutely baffled anyone who knew the family.

They decided that until further paperwork went through and until all the competing bureaucracies sorted themselves out, Peter would have to go *back* to Romaniv. Everyone who knew Peter understood that this would shatter his trust forever. It would be unspeakably devastating. But the decision had been made. One year after leaving Romaniv Disabled Boys Orphanage, Peter was forced to return.

I remember hearing this news for the first time. I was shocked. What would this do to Peter's new foundation of hope? Wasn't being abandoned again the one thing he had always feared? Would Peter ever trust again? I admit that I began to feel a sense of numb helplessness about the whole situation. I thought this story already had a happy ending. How could this happen?

But for Yuri, Peter's new father, numb helplessness never entered into the equation. For him, the whole situation boiled down to one simple fact: "My son needs me. I will not abandon him." So, in a move that left the jaws of the state officials on the ground, Yuri did the only thing he could think to do. He packed his bags, set up a cot, and moved into Romaniv Orphanage *with* Peter. He didn't know how long he would be living there. He didn't know how it would end. But for a dedicated father whose son was in need, Yuri didn't even think twice.

In a country where conforming to the norm is often valued above all else, Yuri's bold move put a lot of pressure on the state officials. Fearing a public spectacle, the officials quickly "found" the lost paperwork, attained the correct signatures, and finally allowed Peter to return to his rightful home. After three days, Peter was once again taken out of Romaniv. This time, however, something was different. This time, Peter's adoption was permanent.

On April 30th, 2010, Peter came home... For good.

Peter with his family in 2010

Two months after this second homecoming, I had the chance to have dinner with Yuri, Ira, and the kids. We laughed and played and talked. We ate and ate and ate. And as I looked across the room at the wide, beautiful smile on Peter's face, I knew I was being given a glimpse of God's heart for the world.

In the banquet of the kingdom, the broken of the world are honored guests. The outcast and forgotten are sons. And there sat Peter. A full tummy. A clean body. And eyes that sparkled with joy.

—

For the next few years, Peter's body continued to weaken, but his love and faith continued to grow. Most people expected the muscular dystrophy to reach his heart or liver and end his life quickly, but he remained inexplicably resilient. His extended life baffled doctors.

According to Yuri, this was because of a divine visitation Peter experienced one night early into his days with the new family. As Peter explained to Yuri one morning, he had been visited by Jesus in the night.

"Oh yeah?" Yuri asked when he heard this. "What did he say?"

"He said it was time for me to go with him," Peter replied. "He wanted to take me home."

"And how did you reply?" Yuri asked.

"I said, 'Well, I'm actually really happy here. Is it OK if I stay a bit longer?' So Jesus said, 'Sure. I'll come back later.'"

Was this simply a dream Peter had or was it a real face to face conversation with Jesus? I suppose there is no way to know for sure. All I know is that Peter went on to live *years* longer than anyone ever predicted.

———

In the summer of 2014, after five delightful years in the arms of a loving family, Peter's body started to quickly decline. He told his parents he was ready to be with Jesus, and on July 1, Peter passed away quietly in the night.

When I heard the news, I wept tears of grief mingled with tears of joy. As much as my heart broke to hear of Peter's death, I also found myself rejoicing. Peter's broken body is now made whole. He was now in the arms of his *heavenly* father. And some day, when I too pass away, I will be reunited with my dear friend, Peter, whose joy and humor and life was an inspiration to everyone who met him.

A few months after Peter's funeral, I had the chance to visit his burial site with Yuri and Peter's big brother Taras. We stood quietly around the grave, still covered in colorful wreaths and streamers. After a time of prayer, we began to reminisce about Peter's life and the many ways he had inspired everyone around him. Finally, we got back into Yuri's van and drove back to Zhytomyr.

As I watched the tall birch trees scrolling by, I thought back to the way I ended the blog post announcing Peter's official adoption back in 2010.

Peter is home now. Though his body is weak and he may not have much longer to live, he will spend the rest of his days wrapped in the arms of a loving family. And when he does some day leave this broken world, he will be well used to the phrase he hears soon after. "My beloved son... Welcome home."

16

Cesar

When I am weak, then I am strong.

My head was spinning as I walked out the door. I looked around at the overcast sky, the tall trees, and the muddy pathway in front of me and shook my head. It was like emerging from a dream. For the last hour, I had been on the receiving end of a fire hose of scripture, prophecy, challenges, encouragement, and prayer from one of the most godly, Spirit-filled men of faith I'd ever met.

He spoke of his deep gratitude for God's provision. He shared his hopes and dreams for both this life and the one to come. He shared passage after passage of scripture from memory. After hearing him share, my perspective on thankfulness was forever changed.

Who was this man? Some globe-trotting evangelist? A famous pastor? Perhaps a professor at a Bible college? Nope. His name was Cesar. He was poor, he was paralyzed, and he lived in constant pain. Yet despite the fact he had no idea how much longer he would live, despite the fact he couldn't provide for his family, and despite the fact he was confined to his bed,

Cesar was a man of deep gratitude. You read that correctly. Cesar, a paralyzed Guatemalan farmer, was *thankful* for the things God had done.

I first heard about Cesar during my initial visit to Saber y Gracia, an elementary school in rural Guatemala, in 2013. His three children were in the school's sponsorship program, and my new friends Lauren and Rudi had told me he was someone I needed to meet. So one afternoon we piled into Rudi's car and headed over to Cesar's bright orange home on the edge of Santo Tomás.

We entered the house, greeted Cesar's wife and three delightful children, and took a seat by the side of his bed. After exchanging a few introductions, he just launched right in, sharing his testimony with an urgency and passion I didn't immediately understand.

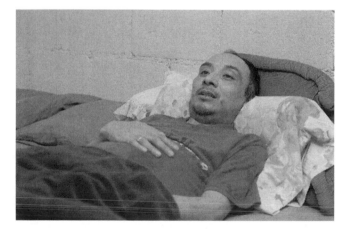

Cesar in 2014

Because Cesar couldn't turn his head, and because I happened to be sitting at the foot of his bed, he looked my direction during most of our conversation. As he quoted scriptures, shared encouragements, and challenged us in our faith, I couldn't help but feel like he was talking specifically to me.

At one point he looked me right in the eyes and quoted 1 Thessalonians 5:18. "Give thanks in all circumstances, for this is God's will for you in Christ Jesus." After reciting the verse, he repeated passionately, "Be grateful in everything. Be grateful in everything."

It was a moment I will never forget. All I could do was sit in stunned silence. Knowing what his life had been like up to that point, it simply didn't make any sense. I remember thinking, *What in the world does Cesar have to be grateful for?!?*

———

Twelve years ago, Cesar was a healthy, hard-working farmer trying to make ends meet for his young family. One day, however, he noticed something was wrong. He began experiencing pains throughout his body as he worked.

Visits to multiple doctors revealed that Cesar had a rare and awful condition that caused his bones to slowly fuse together. Three years later, he could no longer work and was confined to his bed, paralyzed over much of his body and in great pain.

Making matters worse, Cesar's condition was degenerative. As time passed, he lost more and more of his ability to operate his limbs. On the day I first visited him, Cesar could only move his eyes, his mouth, and his right hand. I can't think of a more awful way to live. Not only was he in great pain, not only did he have an uncertain future, but he had absolutely no ability to care for himself and had to face the daily indignities of helplessness and dependence. And yet, as he spoke with us, it was clear he wasn't just paying lip service to the concept of gratitude. His thankfulness seemed to permeate every fiber of his being.

For example, he explained that he was grateful God gave him such a wonderful wife who had stuck with him over many difficult years. He was grateful as well that God had provided an education for his children, despite the fact that he couldn't work. He was grateful that friends from the US donated and built a new house for his family.

But Cesar's gratitude went one step deeper than that. He wasn't just grateful for things that had come about *in spite of* his illness. He was grateful for the illness itself.

What in the world? How could anyone be grateful for such a horrific condition? My confusion continued until Cesar recited 2 Corinthians 12:8-10 from memory (the way he did with every Bible verse. The guy was a machine).

Three times I pleaded with the Lord to take it away from me. But he said to me, "My grace is sufficient for you, for my power is made perfect in weakness." Therefore I will boast all the more gladly about my weaknesses, so that Christ's power may rest on me. That is why, for Christ's sake, I delight in weaknesses, in insults, in hardships, in persecutions, in difficulties. For when I am weak, then I am strong.

After reciting the verse, Cesar continued, "So that's truth, that's real. When I have pain in my body a lot of times at night or early morning, that's when I can feel God's power over me and he holds me in his arms. He says, 'My son you are beloved; rest in my grace.'"

Wow. Cesar was grateful for his illness because it is through weakness that Christ is strong. Cesar was grateful that his illness forced him to rely on God in ways he never had to before. He was grateful that his illness had given him time to meditate on the truths of God's Word. He was grateful that his illness had brought him in contact with believers from all around the world. And he was grateful that he now had a platform to share the gospel with his neighbors. He told us, "I used to have to pound down their doors to talk about Jesus. Now they come to visit *me* and I can talk about him all I want!"

Cesar understood something I never fully did before, and it's this – his condition made him weak in his own power, but *strong* in Christ's.

As we came to the end of our time together, Cesar sang us one of his favorite hymns, then prayed over our group. I was stunned as I thought about what I was witnessing. In an impoverished community far from my home, at the bedside of a weak and helpless paralytic, I was in the presence of one of the most powerful people of faith I've ever met.

When I am weak, then I am strong.

Now *that* is something to be grateful for.

17

Abundance

That's a heck of a lot of cows.

During my year in Kenya in 2005, I spent a few months living in a newly constructed apartment on the edge of Nairobi. The place was nothing fancy. With shoddy construction and a complete lack of furniture, it wasn't exactly the essence of comfort for my roommates and me. But the complex did have a gate with guards, and the windows all had bars on them for security, so at least I didn't have to worry about my single plastic chair getting stolen.

Despite my humble living situation, I found myself struggling with some serious guilt. Just outside the apartment complex, mere feet from the front gate, was a small slum community. Perhaps fifty or a hundred families lived in tin-roofed shacks at the end of the road. To enter my apartment complex I had to essentially walk through the entrance to the slum every single day. It also meant that I could see deeply impoverished people every time I looked out my window.

The longer I lived there the guiltier I felt. Every shilling I spent on myself made me feel like more and more of a selfish pig. How could I live with so much when my *literal* neighbors were stuck in pervasive poverty? It got to the point where I could barely spend anything at all. My meals were bread with peanut butter. I drank only water. I vividly remember picking up a small bunch of bananas at the grocery store, then putting them back, convincing myself it was an unnecessary expense.

You'd think that all this "selfless" living would have resulted in me giving much more away, but this spending paralysis wasn't replaced with material generosity. Not at all. The money I received from my internship stipend each month just started piling up in my closet. I was wracked with guilt, and nobody was the better because of it.

Something snapped inside of me during that season of my life, and it remained broken when I came home to suburban Indianapolis. Even without a constant reminder of the world's poverty in front of me, I could barely buy even generic-brand groceries for myself without guilt creeping in. I wasn't able to enjoy much of anything, especially "luxuries," because I couldn't shake the feeling that I was doing something wrong.

At some point in this season, however, I read the book *God's Smuggler*, by Brother Andrew. The book is his autobiographical account of smuggling Bibles through the Iron Curtain and living in absolute dependence on God for even his most basic of needs. It's a phenomenal story, and it fired me up to be more fully surrendered to God. But one section of the book hit me right in the gut and changed my perspective on money forever.

After getting married, Brother Andrew and his wife began to notice their frugality and simplicity slipping, as mine was, into something more extreme. He describes the two of them discovering "a whole pattern of poverty into which we had fallen, a dark, brooding, pinched attitude that hardly went with the Christ of the open heart that we were preaching to others." He and his wife had come to learn that God really is a father, just as displeased with a cramped "attitude of lack" as he is with "acquisitiveness."

This struck a serious chord in my heart. Brother Andrew was describing *me*. I had slipped into a spirit of poverty. I was living as if God didn't have the power to take care of me *and* those who were struggling with material lack elsewhere in the world. My self-effacing spending habits weren't honoring God. They were questioning his generosity.

In the wake of this realization, I began a long journey to seek equilibrium between living simply and actually *enjoying* life. I allowed myself to eat out a bit more often with friends. I gave myself permission to start saving a small portion of my income to buy nice things like camping gear and computers from time to time. To my surprise, my *giving* began to increase as well, springing out of a newfound spirit of abundance that was beginning to put down roots in my heart.

I imagine I will always be frugal - it's kind of hard-wired into me - but I can now say with confidence that I am no longer a miser. I believe God has "cattle on a thousand hills" (Psalm 50:10), and that he takes great delight in giving his children good things. So I have chosen to hold on to my money with open hands. By remembering who owns it all, I am free to live simply, give generously, and enjoy the world I live in.

18

Relief

In my defense, the camping knife was super cool.

One day in February of 2010, I found myself digging a hole with an elderly Haitian man. Or more accurately, I found myself frantically *trying* to dig a hole while the man and his friends laughed at me. I had seen the man attempting to put a tent pole into the ground, so I offered to try myself. Even though I only had a roll of duct tape and my large camping knife with me, I insisted on giving it a shot.

I started stabbing the hard ground while using my free hand to sweep the loose dirt away. It *kind of* worked. After about five minutes, I had dug an eight inch deep hole and worked up a furious sweat in the hot Caribbean sun. The man and his friends watched the whole thing with amusement. I must have looked like a complete idiot, attacking the ground like a madman with so little to show for my work. I stood up, wiped the sweat from my forehead and smiled sheepishly, completely confident that I had done roughly *zero* good for the guy, but hopeful that at least the gesture would be appreciated.

Exhausted and a bit embarrassed, I gave the man my roll of duct tape, snapped a few photos, and started walking back to join the rest of my team. As I reached the top of the hill where they were working, I looked back at where I had just been. We were in the middle of a makeshift tent camp on the banks of a dried-out riverbed. Hundreds, if not thousands, of displaced refugees had begun moving into the area and setting up shelters out of whatever materials they could find; sticks, trash, tarps, metal scraps, etc.

I was feeling quite useless in the face of so much need, and stabbing a hole in the dirt did little to make me feel valuable. Unfortunately, the rest of my team, who *did* have valuable skills to offer, were struggling with similar sentiments.

I had hitched a ride to Haiti with a medical team organized by our host organization, Nehemiah Vision Ministries. It was just two weeks after the disastrous earthquake brought Port-au-Prince to its knees. Our plan was to use an old school bus as a mobile clinic, visiting communities of earthquake survivors and addressing the many medical emergencies caused by the disaster. The doctors, nurses, and pharmacists on the team were great people, eager to offer relief and aid, but this trip was not going the way any of us had expected.

When we first loaded up the mobile clinic, the team brought supplies and gear for what it would most likely encounter: amputations, internal bleeding, open wounds, etc. Because so much rubble and debris were flying around during the quake, we expected it to be pretty grim. The medical professionals on our team were mentally prepared to address the carnage and I, as a writer and photographer, had steeled myself to capture it all. I was ready to tell compelling stories to my readers back home, regardless of how uncomfortable it would make me.

Imagine our team's surprise, then, at what medical problems we ended up addressing: venereal disease, respiratory infections, and stomach ailments. One person after another came to get help for problems that had nothing to do with the earthquake. These were not the horrific results of a natural disaster. These were the everyday medical problems of *poverty*. It didn't take long for frustration to set in. These were doctors who gave up vacation time to do earthquake relief. They came to save people's lives. They didn't come to prescribe antibiotics for intestinal infections.

The hastily constructed riverbank tent camp

As patient after patient came in to have a rash looked at or a cough listened to or an STD treated, it became clear we were trying to put a Band-Aid on a gaping wound. There were far more medical needs in just this tiny refugee camp than we could ever hope to address. The line to see our doctors stretched hundreds of feet down the hill. At the end of the day we turned many people away. Our team's tireless efforts were little more than a drop in a giant bucket of poverty. It was kind of like me stabbing the dirt for a tent pole when an entire community needed a place to sleep that night.

This one experience proved to be part of a much larger phenomenon I've seen played out over and over again around the world. American teams, eager to address the needs of the poor and marginalized, *excel* at relief. We're great at fixing problems and using creative improvisations to help those in trouble. Case in point: our medical team set up a fully functional medical clinic in an old, converted *school bus*. Impressive.

But there are times when the primary need in an impoverished community is not relief, but *development*. Long-term, strategic programs need to be started. Multi-generational education initiatives need to be invested in. Indigenous leaders need to be raised up and trained.[6]

To truly help the people in the refugee camp that day and set them on a course to be free from poverty, we would have needed to address issues of employment, childhood education, agricultural sustainability, potable water, community leadership, spiritual development, youth empowerment, *and* medical care. And not just one of these things at a time, but *all of them* at once. And not just on a couple of short term trips, but over *decades*.

Frankly, just *imagining* all of that is exhausting. And to be honest, it leaves me feeling a bit numb.

Thankfully, over the last six years or so I've stumbled onto a beautiful solution to this quandary, and it's this: getting out of the way and letting local leaders shine. What I mean is, we can make space for indigenous, local leaders to take point on the development of their own communities. We can stop calling the shots and start supporting those who are already there.

These local leaders are in it for the long haul. They're not going home after their short term trip is over. They *are* home. Do they have years of training and education and know-how for the work God has called them to do? Probably not. But they *do* have something we as Americans can't hope to achieve without years in the field - deep cultural understanding, fluency in the language, and the trust of their neighbors.

Now, I realize this may seem overly simplistic. And it

---

[6] For a phenomenal, in-depth look at this concept, check out the book *When Helping Hurts* by Brian Fikkert and Steve Corbett.

probably is to some degree. There will always be a need for the skill and expertise of trained professionals to tackle the world's greatest injustices. But as I've traveled, I've seen more and more problems in which the solution is not actually relief, but *development*, and the people best suited to long-term, sustainable development are the "long-haulers" who are already there.

———

At the end of our frustrating day in the tent camp, the medical team and I piled into the mobile clinic/bus and drove back to Pastor Pierre's home on the outskirts of town. We showered, ate some dinner, then hung out around the house, killing some time before bed. At one point, while idly leaning on the balcony, I looked down into the living room below. There, completely passed out on the couch with a three ring binder laying open on his chest, was Pastor Pierre.

Esperandieu Pierre, who had founded our host ministry, Nehemiah Vision Ministries, a few years earlier, had been working non-stop since the earthquake. Born into poverty himself, Pierre had the opportunity to study abroad. But instead of leaving his country forever, he chose to return and work tirelessly for the empowerment of other Haitians. After his nation was plunged into chaos, Pierre dove straight into action.

While I was stabbing the dirt in a refugee camp, Pierre was using every resource at his disposal to get aid shipments released from customs, to coordinate new construction at NVM's main campus, and to juggle the many churches, non-profits, and individuals who were eager to help in some way, all while pastoring frightened people who had just experienced the most traumatic natural disaster in their nation's history. Yes, we were both exhausted after a long day, but in that moment I felt like he had actually *earned* a little shuteye.

As I thought about his relentless work ethic and drive, I realized something significant. Pastor Pierre wasn't going anywhere. Although I'd be boarding a plane bound for home just a few days later, Pierre would still be there, working his fingers to the bone to help the people of his nation.

As I write this, nearly five years after my day in the riverbank camp, Esperandieu Pierre continues his work in Haiti. NVM has continued to grow, and now reaches thousands of people with life-sustaining medical help, empowering education, and faith-filled spiritual guidance. They are slowly, but steadily *transforming* their community, and have been gradually expanding their reach to help other communities as well.

Although there may have been very little good done by our mobile medical clinic's stint outside the tent camp that day, I am confident Pastor Pierre and the other indigenous leaders he's raised up will be changing the nation of Haiti for decades to come. This is just one example of why I believe we need a paradigm shift in our approach to global aid. Instead of enlisting local leaders to help *us* in our mission, it's time to come alongside *them* with the support and resources they need to change their own communities for the long-haul.

It may not be the easiest, simplest, or fastest way to see results, but let's be real. It's *way* better than stabbing the dirt.

19

Malaika

Well, I think my arms are quite angelic.

While I was living in my Nairobi apartment in 2005, my forearms became pretty popular. As I mentioned before, the gate into the apartment complex shared the end of the road with a small slum community. The apartment was new and relatively nice, but the location of the gate meant I pretty much had to walk through the entrance to the slum to get home.

Since there were very few *mzungus* (white people) in the area, it became a mini event every time I walked up to the gate. Kids would run out of the slum yelling "Mzungu! How are you?" over and over. Occasionally I'd kick a soccer ball around with them or play a quick game of tag.

As the kids got more comfortable with me, they sometimes surrounded me and started rubbing my arm hair. Most Kenyan men have smooth arms, so this was quite a unique experience for them. They would crowd around, rubbing their hands up and down my hairy arms. As they did this, they would get serious, trance-like looks in their eyes and stare up at me, repeating the word "Malaika, malaika, malaika…"

I found the whole experience a bit odd, so one day I decided to ask one of my Kenyan friends, Milton, what was going on.

"Hey, Milton. What does *malaika* mean?" I asked.

"It means angel," he replied.

Woah. Angel?!? I thought. *They think I am an angel because of my white skin? What does that say about the clash of Western and African cultures? What does that say about the status of education for impoverished families in Nairobi? What does that say about…*

"It also means arm hair," Milton continued.

"Oh," I replied. "Right… thanks. Good to know. Good to know."

20

The Sapling

But again, it's a great place to lose weight.

"Did you enjoy your time in South Sudan?"

I stood in the guesthouse living room, looking into the eyes of my interpreter, Santino. It was my last night in the country and we were saying our goodbyes.

Did I enjoy my time in South Sudan? I didn't know how to answer. Santino looked at me expectantly while my mind ran through a list of the things I'd experienced over the last four weeks: extreme heat, constant sweat, scarce electricity, bucket baths, dirty water, rats, cockroaches, wasps, a stomach infection, endless teeth-rattling car rides on dirt roads, and glacially slow Internet connections. Oh, and did I mention the crushing poverty, widespread corruption, and broken education system?

"Um, Santino? I need to be honest with you," I replied. "No. I did not enjoy my time in South Sudan. But I am so glad I came."

Santino stared at me with a confused look on his face. I

realize how crazy I sounded. If my time in South Sudan was so miserable, why in the world would I be glad I came? After such a difficult month, shouldn't I just shake the dust off my feet, move on and call it a day? Why in the world would I feel grateful for an experience that easily qualifies as the most uncomfortable month of my life?

The only way I can explain it is through a single word: hope. I had hope for the people of South Sudan. After four weeks in that country, I knew God was moving in a powerful way. I'd seen a side of the kingdom of God that most people will never get to see. And I was grateful for this fresh new perspective.

But I'll shoot straight with you. That hope wasn't easy to find. And I might have missed it entirely, if it wasn't for three things: a sweaty pillow, a dirty puddle, and cow theft.

Let me explain.

———

My first taste of South Sudan came the moment I stepped off the plane. A furnace-blast of heat hit me like a brick wall. I had a farmer's tan within seconds. Antiperspirant companies started calling to ask if I'd star in their new commercials. Let's just say it was hot.

After picking my way through the crowded and chaotic airport, I found my ride: Lawrence and Sunday, two staff members of African Leadership and Reconciliation Ministries (ALARM), my host ministry for the month.

As we drove through the capital, Juba, I was struck by how run down and weary everything looked. At one point, Sunday pointed out her window and said, "That's the rich part of town. Only very wealthy people live there." I looked where she pointed to see a few walls topped with broken glass and a smoldering trash heap.

OK, I thought. *This is going to be… different.*

We wound our way through late-morning traffic and into Gudele, a community on the edge of Juba. Looking at Gudele on a map, all you can see is an endless grid of dirt roads and homes stretching off in every direction. The neighborhood went from uninhabited bush to sprawling suburb in less than two years, a microcosm of the greater rural to urban shift happening in the country. Since independence in 2011, the new capital of Juba had become a major economic hub. People from all over the new nation had flocked to the city in search of prosperity.

But that doesn't mean they'd found it.

We finally arrived at the house where I'd be living during my month in South Sudan. We walked into the dark building and Lawrence opened the door to a bedroom. He poked his head in and said, "Here's where you'll be staying."

I looked around the room. A single window, covered in metal bars for security, provided the only source of light. There wasn't much to illuminate. A bed, a mosquito net, a footstool, and a large, industrial-size fan were the only pieces of furniture in the room.

It was pretty hot and steamy inside, but I was relieved to see the fan. As long as I had that, I was sure I could handle the heat. Little did I know I was about to receive my first lesson about the realities of life in South Sudan.

As I quickly discovered, the infrastructure in the new nation was almost non-existent. At last count before my visit, there were less than 40 miles of paved roads in the entire country. After years of heavy rains, the "highways" between cities looked more like dirt-bike tracks.

Because the country was landlocked and the roads were notoriously bad, fuel was astronomically expensive. At one gas station, I worked out the price for fuel to be around $12 a gallon (this in a country where the main export was *oil*!).

Since there was literally no power grid to draw from, almost all of the electricity in Juba came from individual diesel generators. Thus, electricity in South Sudan was a luxury, and I had to get used to using it only 1-2 hours each evening. The big fan in my room? Nothing more than a decoration 22 hours a day.

Long story short, I got really good at sleeping in a pool of my own sweat. My room was stifling. 85-90 degrees at night. I slept in 3-hour increments. Each night, I woke up multiple times to roll over to the dry side of the bed and swap out my dripping wet foam pillow for a relatively dry one. I don't know if you can call it "beauty sleep," but I did lose a ton of weight.

The highlight of every morning was my shower, when I could wash the night's sweat off my body with a bucket of murky water from a basin outside. Although there was a "bathroom" (a moldy closet with a drain in the ground), there was no running water. Another lesson I quickly learned: the country had yet to develop a water or sewage system of any kind.

———

As the month went on, I found myself wondering why the infrastructure of South Sudan was so broken. I mean, the country had areas of very fertile farmland. The massive oil fields were a resource just waiting to be exploited. Sure, being landlocked is a challenge for any country, but Rwanda was landlocked and it was one of the fastest growing economies in Africa. Why was South Sudan so underdeveloped?

This was a question I asked myself over and over as I traveled around the country. From the cool, green south to the hot, arid north, South Sudan seemed mired in an insurmountable swamp of injustice. I couldn't wrap my head around it.

But then I had a realization – a small "aha" moment that helped me understand the reasons behind South Sudan's lack of development. It happened during my visit to the small northern village of Lietnhom.

Lietnhom was just about as poor of a place as you can get. Located smack in the middle of the dry northern regions of South Sudan, most villagers there struggled to get by on a few staple crops and expensive shipments of food from other parts of the country. Although many of the people I met had relatively substantial wealth in cattle, they still struggled with disease, crime, and a lack of education.

The civil war with the north (which had only just ended in 2005) continued to take its toll. Because it was so close to the border, the village of Lietnhom was hit hard by the fighting. It was still in the process of rebuilding.

One day, my friend Kazito, one of the pastors being trained by ALARM, took me to see how people in the region gather water when they don't have access to wells. He had described people collecting water from large pits in the ground and I was intrigued to see what he meant.

As the afternoon began to cool into evening, we hopped on his motorcycle. Zipping down narrow dirt paths, we passed huts, cows, and numerous naked toddlers, staring in bewilderment at the *khawaja* (white guy) hanging on for dear life.

Finally, we pulled up to a large depression in the ground about 60 feet in diameter. We walked up to the lip of the crater and looked into the pit below. A woman in a faded blue dress stood waist deep in a muddy hole, holding a plastic container filled with murky water.

As I watched, she crouched down with a small cup and skimmed a bit of relatively clear water off the top of a brown puddle. She poured the water into a plastic bucket and repeated the process. This, I realized, was the water she and her family would use to drink, cook and clean that evening.

"This is bad," Kazito said, shaking his head. "This water is no good."

Yeah, no kidding, I thought.

As we drove to several other water pits and met other women collecting muddy, parasite-infested water for their families, I asked Kazito why people didn't just sell a cow or two to pay for a legitimate well.

First, he explained, the only way it would work is for several families to pitch in together. Getting drilling equipment to such a remote region was expensive. But nobody would do that because they didn't want to give up a single cent of their precious wealth (i.e. their cows).

"Don't they realize the health of their families would be worth the investment?" I asked.

"They don't have enough education to understand the

causes of disease," Kazito explained.

I kept at it. "Why don't village elders band together to get the entire community engaged?"

In essence, Kazito told me, there was too much corruption for local leaders to work together.

"What about non-profits? Foreign aid? The government?"

Kazito stared at me. "What organization will spend thousands of dollars to bring clean water to a handful of families in the desert?"

Some of the women Kazito and I met outside Lietnhom

This was when it hit me. This pattern of seemingly insurmountable problems - I'd seen it before. The unemployed fathers in Juba who couldn't afford to send their kids to school. The war-orphaned street kids in Yei scraping by with odd jobs to feed their younger siblings. The corrupt officials who expected me to pay them a bribe at the Wau bus station.

Each one of these problems was a part of a larger cycle. Each one fed into another aspect of poverty, and was itself fed by hunger, disease and crime. But these weren't small-scale problems. These weren't just mini-injustices expressing themselves in individual communities. I was seeing the effects of an entire country trapped in the cycle of poverty.

It was like the light had turned on. Standing at the edge of a pit on the outskirts of a remote village, my eyes were opened. This was more than just a lack of clean water for one family. This muddy water was connected to a lack of education which was connected to a broken agricultural system which was connected to a struggling export economy which was connected to an abysmal highway system which was connected to a lack of electricity which was connected to corrupt government officials. On and on it went.

This was one of the most comprehensive cycles of poverty I'd ever seen.

———

All of a sudden I had a new context to understand the realities I'd witnessed throughout the country. High infant mortality led to an unsustainable birth rate, illness and malnutrition led to a lack of education, and because of cultural norms, even those who did earn a livable income inevitably got sucked right back into poverty by having to care for their whole extended family.

In South Sudan, *the entire country* was caught in the cycle.

My only option for finding hope was to dig in and try to understand what ALARM was doing in the country. I had just seen their tremendous work in Rwanda, so I was sure some good stuff would be happening in South Sudan as well. At least, I hoped it was.

Like their ministry in Rwanda, I assumed ALARM would be doing a lot of community development work in South Sudan: things like trade schools, micro-finance initiatives, childhood education, that sort of thing. And they *were* doing this to some degree, but most of the work ALARM was doing in South Sudan focused simply on training pastors.

I wanted to see this work firsthand, so I spent a week visiting ALARM's main training school, the Christian Leadership Institute of South Sudan (CLISS) in Yei. My visit happened to be during one of their training sessions, so I got to see what these pastors from around the country were learning.

The town of Yei was green, peaceful and about 15 degrees cooler than Juba. After sweating like a wookie in a sauna for two weeks, the change of scenery was heavenly. But after meeting some of the pastors and sitting in on a couple of their classes, I found myself a bit confused.

I mean, at first glance, it looked like ALARM was missing the point in South Sudan. Why train pastors with theological concepts when there were people starving? Why educate them in biblical interpretation when violence and insecurity were such pressing social matters? Wasn't it more important to care for people's urgent needs first, and *then* discuss eschatology?

I wondered all of this until I overheard a discussion about cattle rustling. Yes, *that* kind of cattle rustling. The "Garn. Git outta here 'fore I call the sheriff" kind.

———

One sunny afternoon in Yei, I sat down with the CLISS pastors between classes. They were scattered in a loose circle of plastic chairs in the shade of a giant mango tree. I grabbed an empty chair and listened in. By the time I joined them, they were already deep in discussion.

"The Bible says do not steal. Look. Right here in Exodus 20. It's one of the ten commandments. Just tell them that."

"Yes, but they don't believe it's stealing."

"No no no… You're both missing the point. It's *murder* that we should be talking about. That's the real problem here."

I pulled one of the students aside and asked what everyone was discussing. He told me, "We are talking about what to do with cattle rustlers in our congregations."

"Why?" I asked, "Is this a big problem in the church here?"

"Oh, yes. Very much," he told me. "This problem is everywhere."

As the students eventually explained to me, cattle rustling was a major issue in South Sudan, especially within the church. Despite being ostensibly "Christian," many church-goers participated in this illegal act. But it went far deeper than simply stealing cows. In fact, it had a lot to do with weddings. And murder.

Here's how it worked. Getting married in South Sudan was no easy task. The bride-price to be paid to the woman's father was 100 cows, the equivalent of tens of thousands of dollars. Unless a man was very wealthy, he couldn't come close to affording this. So most unmarried men just got jobs and lived with their parents, right? Wrong. You see, most men who weren't married became laughingstocks. In that culture, marriage was in many ways a rite of passage into adulthood.

So what would a desperate man do when he needed 100 cows? Well, he'd steal them from someone else, of course. But there was a problem with this. After decades of civil war, there were *lots* of guns in South Sudan. Many landowners defended their property with automatic weapons. So the potential cattle rustler needed to come prepared. He'd take a bunch of friends with a bunch of guns along with him to do the deed.

It doesn't take much imagination to guess what would happen next. Bullets would be fired. People would be killed. Regardless of who ended up with the cows, murder and death were all too often at the end of this simple crime.

As the discussion continued, the pastors talked about the issue from all angles. They discussed what it would take to change the hearts of young men in their churches. They spoke about the need for discipleship. They even talked about the importance of working with local village leaders to create a comprehensive mandate for lower bride prices.

Although few concrete conclusions were reached in that discussion, I walked away completely astonished. I actually understood. The puzzle pieces finally fit together and I had found the hope I was looking for.

Cattle rustling, murder, corruption, poverty, and violence were all systemic issues. They were cultural and economic and moral problems. No government initiative or international non-profit could fix any one of them. No amount of foreign aid or military intervention or diplomacy was going to break these cycles of injustice.

But these pastors could.

That's what hit me under the mango tree. These pastors –

this ragtag group of poorly educated, unrefined, inexperienced pastors – actually had a shot.

Who else had the capacity to walk alongside community members from their birth to their graves? Who else had both the authority of a leader and the accessibility of a next-door neighbor? Who else had the ear of civic leaders, village elders, and everyday farmers alike? Who else had an existing community structure to draw on for poverty alleviation, education and orphan care?

These pastors were the key. Their churches were the hope I was looking for. And they were the ones ALARM had chosen to invest in.

A few of the pastors being trained by ALARM

All of a sudden, equipping these leaders with biblical interpretation skills didn't seem so out of place. Getting their feet firmly established in theological principles wasn't such a waste of time.

Give these pastors the tools they needed to lead well and their congregations would be transformed. Let these congregations influence their villages and their *communities* would be transformed. Let these communities begin to change their regions, and *South Sudan* would be transformed.

The Local Church is the hope of the world, and these leaders were the tip of the spear.

When I left South Sudan a few weeks after visiting Yei, I held tightly to this powerful hope. It wasn't a lot. I wasn't overflowing with optimism and excitement. But I was confident that ALARM was investing its resources in exactly the right place at exactly the right time.

Now, I won't lie and say I had a blast in South Sudan. Taking a tepid bucket bath with brown river water (and being drenched in sweat again before even toweling off) wasn't my idea of a good time. Generally, I prefer not to have rats jumping on my bed in the middle of the night. I never did learn to enjoy "combo," the slimy green food that looked suspiciously like elephant snot.

But I will never regret the month I spent there. I had the phenomenal privilege of witnessing the early years of a growing spiritual movement. I got to meet leaders who would one day be changing the face of their country's Church.

Some might see a mountain of insurmountable challenges in South Sudan. And they're right to see it that way. But I serve a mountain-*moving* God, and I've met His agents of change.

———

At one point on my trip, I got to meet a young man who had recently settled down on the outskirts of Juba. In his enthusiasm for the future, he had planted two small mango trees on his property. As his kids ran in and out of the house, I asked him how long it would take for the trees to bear fruit.

"Oh, about five or six years," he told me.

Wow. Talk about a long-term view. When I saw them, the saplings were pretty worthless. No fruit. No shade. They weren't even strong enough to support a hammock. But this was only the beginning. In time, the trees would grow.

What a perfect analogy for what God is doing in South Sudan. Like the baby mango trees in the dirt, it may take years to see fruit in this country. But the people of South Sudan are resilient. Despite war and poverty and disease, the kingdom of God is spreading. In the midst of corruption and greed, servant leaders are on the move.

The Church of God is growing in South Sudan. Like a sapling tree, it's spreading its branches to the sky and shooting roots deep into the ground. Powerful leaders are being raised up. Despite setbacks and challenges and financial hurdles, ALARM is pushing forward, making sure this growth continues.

Transformation won't happen overnight. Systems of injustice are stubborn. But one fact remains; the Local Church is the hope of the world, and it's not going anywhere.

21

Living History

Way better than flannel graphs

"Why would anybody put a bath tub on the roof?"

As a young man, this is what I wondered when I heard the story of David and Bathsheba. "I mean, what did Bathsheba *expect* would happen when she took a bubble bath for the whole world to see? I guess her name *does* have the word 'bath' in it, so maybe that's her thing, but still…"

It wasn't until I started traveling in the developing world that I began to understand what was going on here. After taking countless bucket baths in places with no running water, I realized Bathsheba didn't have a cast iron clawfoot bathtub on her roof. She was most likely just bathing out of a basin, the way the *vast majority* of people do in impoverished communities today. The only reason she did it on the roof was because it was the place she'd find the most privacy (well, privacy from *most* eyes at least). Just like that, my entire understanding of that story had changed.

This has happened a lot to me over the years. When I

walked 10 miles through the desert near Somalia with my friend Boniface, it felt totally normal when strangers started to walk alongside us. They'd join us for a few miles, chatting to while away the slow hours spent walking between villages. Looking through the gospels and the book of Acts, this is a pretty common occurrence. It must have happened all the time in the days before HOV lanes.

Living in places with no electricity like rural Panama has given me a new perspective on light. Jesus, for example, talks a *lot* about light and lamps and flame. These illustrations have taken on new significance to me now that I understand how valuable and rare light is in the long, dark hours of the night. Being "the light of the world" is a stunning image when imagining a cloudy, starless night with a single kerosene lamp holding back the darkness.

But of all the places I've been, there is one that feels the most like stepping straight into the pages of the Bible: rural India. Seriously, there are so many similarities between life in an Indian village and Ancient Near Eastern culture, it's ridiculous.

The village of Saddulakheda in northern India is a perfect example. It was the site of a footwashing event hosted by Truthseekers. I got to watch as the villagers who attended the event heard the good news of the gospel for the very first time. It was amazing to see such dignity, life, and pride come over people so downtrodden by their society's expectations. After the Truthseekers team left, I had the amazing opportunity to spend the night in the village with one of Truthseekers' young leaders, Kamalakar Deshpande. He and I spent the rest of the day walking around the community, and I couldn't believe what I was seeing.

The village was made up of one and two story buildings with flat roofs, just like in ancient Israel. The people living there were primarily subsistence farmers, harvesting and threshing rice by hand, using donkeys to carry heavy loads, burning cow droppings for fuel, and sleeping on woven mats. One Bible story after another ran through my head as I saw the settings of Jesus' parables lived out in front of my eyes.

In the fields around Saddulakheda, I met a group of three Gypsy women who owned no land, picking up the stalks of grain that had fallen to the ground when the farmers were harvesting. This was their only way of feeding their family. All of a sudden, the Old Testament command to leave the edges of your fields unharvested for the poor made a whole lot more sense.

For dinner, Deshpande and I sat in the upper room of our host, a "man of peace"[7] who welcomed us to stay in his house for the night, even though we had never met before that day. We ate unleavened bread and curried vegetables with our hands, then sat around talking late into the night with the elders of the village. A homemade kerosene lamp flickered on the wall for light. For hours, the men of the village listened intently as Deshpande spoke persuasively about Jesus. They had never even *heard* of him before. To a community of lower-caste people, oppressed by a deeply-woven system of injustice, the gospel of peace was *incredibly* good news.

We awoke the next morning to the sound of roosters, confident the gospel had been planted in Saddulakheda, and eager to see how God would work in the days ahead. After taking quick bucket baths, Deshpande and I said goodbye to our generous hosts, walked out of the village and started making our way back to Delhi. As we rode the train back to the city, I knew I'd never look at the book of Acts the same way again.

---

[7] This must be what Luke 10:6 meant!

22

Charcoal

I knew there was something fishy about Count Frederico.

While living in Kibera Slum with Pastor Fred's family, I awoke every morning to the sound of something plastic being waved vigorously back and forth.

Whump-a-whump-a-whump-a-whump...

For a few blessed moments, the rhythmic shaking noises were all I could hear - almost like white noise in the background. Then, without fail, babies started crying, radios started blaring, and the hubbub of a hundred voices could be heard through my thin metal walls. Eventually, I got used to the noise, but sleeping in was never a real possibility.

For a while, I couldn't figure out what the shaking noise was that started my morning routine.

Whump-a-whump-a-whump.

It sounded like someone using a frisbee to fan themselves, but I knew that couldn't be it. Kibera in June is actually quite chilly in the mornings - often down into the low 50's Fahrenheit. To the Kenyans I knew, it might as well have been 20 below freezing. I'd walk out of my room in a t-shirt, startled to notice my neighbor wearing a puffy winter jacket.

So it wasn't a frisbee.

One morning, I finally found the answer to the mystery. Up earlier than usual, I stepped into the small alley outside my door to brush my teeth and stumbled across Goretty, my host mother, using a sheet of plastic to fan a small pile of burning charcoal in a ceramic stove (called a "jiko"). She was starting the morning's cook fire. This little pile of charcoal would boil the water our family used to bathe and drink that day, and would then be used to cook breakfast. Walking to the end of the alley with my toothbrush still in my mouth, I passed two other mothers fanning their own charcoal jikos. It was one of the first times I realized just how big of a role charcoal plays in the lives of Kibera's residents.

Every evening, Goretty would light up another pile of charcoal to cook dinner. Meanwhile, Fred and I sat in their cramped living room, played with his sons Fadhili and Fortune, and watched English-dubbed Mexican soap operas on their tiny TV. The shows were a bit out of place inside a crowded East African slum, but it was compelling stuff. You just never knew when Mirabella would discover that the mysterious Count Frederico was *actually* her father's evil twin.

Every few days - depending on which way the wind was blowing - thick, acrid smoke from the jiko drifted into the living room, causing us all to choke and cough. Call it a leap of logic, but this phenomenon may have played a role in the many respiratory infections I developed while living there.

One day I was walking back to Tumaini Church with Pastor Fred after a home visit. We passed a woman selling charcoal. Like all of the other charcoal sellers in Kibera, this woman sold her product by volume, not weight. As a result, she had a row of plastic pails seemingly overflowing with various sized black briquettes.

I had seen such a display many times before, and knew the

sight was deceptive. What looked like a really generous amount of charcoal was really an intricately designed latticework, each piece perfectly supporting the one above it. There was as much empty space inside the pail as possible.

Pastor Fred and I chuckled about the phenomenon. Every charcoal seller did it. Every charcoal buyer *knew* they did it. The practice wasn't fooling anybody, but no small business owner wanted to be the first to change their ways.

"If you just breath on it the whole thing will collapse," he joked.

I laughed, then found myself getting curious. "Why is charcoal such a common fuel source in Kibera?" I asked. "Is it the cheapest?"

Actually, he explained, charcoal could be quite expensive for families with little to no income. Propane, he explained, was far cheaper in the long run.

I was surprised to hear this. "Why don't people just use *gas* for their stoves, then?"

His answer was simple, "Because you have to buy the tank."

I didn't understand why this was such a big deal. We continued the conversation all the way back to Tumaini's office, where we sat and sketched out a few numbers on a scrap of paper. Eventually I started to understand. Even though a family cooking with a gas stove would spend *half* as much money as one using charcoal on a monthly basis (potentially saving the cost of the tank in the first *year!*), almost nobody made the switch.

First of all, buying a propane tank in Kibera is a relatively expensive investment - far more than most residents have lying around. Saving that much money is next to impossible when so many urgent expenses like food, shelter, and clothing are always vying for attention.

But it's even more complicated than that. For someone to actually purchase a propane tank, there would be a level of social stigma as well. Their neighbors would begin to see them as rich. They'd assume they had secret stashes of money lying around. The entire dynamic of their social network would change, something absolutely out of the question for people relying on the good will of their neighbors when times get tough.

With the lack of a saving culture in Kibera and the potential social consequences of making the switch to gas, most families choose to stay with charcoal, despite the cost, hassle, and health repercussions.

Thinking through this tricky situation, I of course started running through a list of potential quick fixes in my head. But thanks to what I had learned from Pastor Fred, I shot down each of my ideas as quickly as they came up.

What if we just donated a bunch of propane tanks? Nobody would want their neighbors to think they were rich. The social support structures are too important to jeopardize.

How about if we started a cost/benefit gas awareness campaign so they'd see the value? That would be great if people in Kibera had a culture of saving money, which they don't. Besides, no bank will open an account for such small amounts of cash.

OK, well what if we began an education initiative about how to save money? Awesome, except most people in Kibera barely have enough for the essentials. Long term saving is not easy when you're living hand-to-mouth.

Before long, I had started to believe there wasn't *any* way for this situation to change. Like so many problems in impoverished areas, this one seemed to have no quick fix. I would have given up hope entirely if Pastor Fred hadn't invited me to attend a meeting with him in the room next door to his office.

Like most such invitations, I wasn't entirely sure what I was attending. I didn't have a whole lot of context. Nevertheless, I entered the small classroom and took a seat in a circle made up of Tumaini's teachers and pastors. The meeting had already begun, so I simply sat quietly and observed.

From what I could tell, they were going in a circle, naming different amounts of money, while one participant kept track in a large notebook. When one person didn't name an amount, everyone else gave them a hard time. There was a lot of laughing and good natured teasing. At some point, everyone handed money to the bookkeeper, who put it in his bag for safekeeping. I'll be honest: I had no idea what was going on. But after the meeting was over, Pastor Fred explained it all to me.

The meeting was a grassroots savings and loan group. These twelve people gathered weekly to contribute to a group fund. The amount of money they had collectively was big enough to open a shared bank account. Although each group member's money was still fully theirs, they had to apply to the rest of the group to make a withdrawal. Thus, the communal nature of these relationships added a layer of accountability not present in personal savings.

This may not seem particularly exciting, but I left the meeting completely fired up. Here was the solution to the charcoal problem and many other problems like it! The members of this savings group had become the social safety net for each other. The public accountability was a strong motivator towards saving money. And the shared pool of funds gave the possibility of banking, something they would have never been able to access on their own. If any of these group members decided to buy a propane tank, they now had the capacity to make that happen.

The best thing of all of this was that it had nothing to do with aid. There were no international charities giving handouts. There were no donations involved at all. This was an initiative made possible by local leaders like Pastor Fred. It was a group of people taking ownership of their own lives, and relying on the strength of their community to raise their own standard of living.

Would it bring an end to poverty overnight? Of course not. This was an initiative that would take years to bear real fruit. But for the first time, I actually had hope that change was possible, not from a series of fancy quick fix ideas, but from the hard work of the very people whose lives had the most potential to be changed.

23

Sewa Ashram

To us this place is heaven.

In late 2008, while I was in New Delhi, India, I had the chance to spend a day at Sewa Ashram, a center for the dying and destitute on the outskirts of the giant city. It was a place very similar in purpose to Mother Theresa's ministry in Calcutta. Every day, the Sewa Ashram team drove the streets of New Delhi looking for sick, outcast, starving, dying people, and brought them to their property for medical care, rest, and love.

By the time Sewa Ashram's guests arrived, many were too far gone to resuscitate. The medical staff and volunteers were often helpless to fix their situations. Instead, they simply offered comfort, peace, and tender words as the resident prepares to die.

When I first arrived, I felt quite apprehensive. I expected it to be a place of chaos, noise, and disorder. I pictured people screaming and moaning, stretchers scattered about, and lots of people weeping. As I walked through the main gate, however, I was immediately taken aback by how peaceful the place was. After the hustle and bustle of Delhi, it came as a quite a shock to see a quiet vegetable garden with a pen full of rabbits, a litter of newborn puppies running around, and countless butterflies darting in and out of the shrubs lining the path.

And then there were the smiles. Everywhere I went people seemed to be happy. Patients on death's door had looks of contentment on their faces. Even in the tuberculosis ward, men were chit-chatting, laughing, and generally just having a good time.

None of it seemed to fit. There were grins and laughter from people who were the absolute definition of destitution. In the children's area, for example, I met a boy with spinal tuberculosis, who would never be able to use his legs. I talked to another who had childhood arthritis, bent over due to the pain. Some children were mentally disabled. Others had HIV. And yet all of them seemed full of joy.

One of the young men, who everyone called "Helicopter," was picked up off the street at a very young age. He practically grew up at Sewa Ashram. While other kids ran around us, he leaned on his crutch, smiled, and proudly told me, "I am a child of God, and that means I am taken care of. God always takes care of his children!"

"He sure does," I mumbled, wondering if I truly believed that in the midst of such brokenness.

Towards the end of my tour of the compound, I met a sick and massively malnourished man who couldn't have weighed more than 50 pounds. He reminded me of photos I'd seen from Nazi concentration camps. I could see his bones stretching against his skin, a giant white t-shirt hung from his shoulders like a bed sheet. He sat cross-legged on a woven cot and gave me a smile as I came up to say 'hello.'

My interpreter helped me ask a few questions about the man's life. My mind was spinning so much at the sight of such tremendous human frailty, I don't even remember his answers. All I remember is what he said when I asked what he thought of Sewa Ashram.

"To us," he said, "this place is heaven."

At that, I pretty much lost it. I was moments away from becoming a sobbing, snotty mess. Not sure what else to do, I asked if I could pray for him. He agreed. I put my hand around his bony shoulder, choked back tears, and did my best to say something meaningful to God.

I spent the rest of the day simply hanging out with some of the guests at Sewa Ashram. I sat on a cot and watched two TB patients play a card game. I flew a kite with a wheelchair-bound boy in a nearby field. With my complete language barrier and no discernible medical skills to offer, I simply spent time with people at the absolute bottom rung of society's ladder. When it was over, I took the long bus ride back into town, staring out the window and wrestling with a heart full of conflicting emotions. It was a massively significant experience in my life.

That night, when I returned to my room in New Delhi, I started writing a blog post about the day. As I reached the conclusion of the article, I sat in front of my computer with tears streaming down my face. It was a holy moment in which God was reminding me of just who I was and why I existed. I ended my article with these words:

I will spend myself on behalf of the poor. I will stand beside the broken. And someday, when I stand at his throne, I will know with all of my heart that I spent my life with Jesus.

Just a couple of weeks after this experience, the vision for World Next Door was born.

24

Volcán de Agua

Sweaty backpack meat... What's the worst that could happen?

The first time I came to Guatemala, I felt compelled to climb it: Volcán de Agua, a towering peak dominating the landscape around the city of Antigua. I don't know why. I'd never climbed a mountain before. I'd barely ever been above 6000 feet. It was just there, and practically begged to be conquered.

So I threw the idea out there with my hosts at Saber y Gracia, and to my surprise, they agreed. We gathered a group of teachers and students, drove out to the village of Santa Maria de Jesús at the base of the volcano, and started to climb. It was an unforgettable experience.

The trek started easily enough. Looking up at the peak from our starting point of 6700 feet, I thought, "Sure. How hard can it be?" I mean, I could see the top right there. I couldn't imagine how it could possibly take us more than, say, three or four hours to reach the summit. So, with boundless enthusiasm and energy, my Guatemalan hiking companions and I began scampering up the path. We passed countless farms growing lettuce, beans, and coffee on the gradually steepening slope of the volcano. The sun was bright, but a cool breeze kept us refreshed.

Volcán de Agua, dominating the horizon of the nearby village of Santo Tomás Milpas Altas

After an hour of hiking, we emerged into a clearing and collapsed on a hillside for a breather, smiling and joking about how tired we already were. That's when I saw it. The volcano. Reaching to the sky ahead of me. It hadn't moved an inch. Sure, the peak was *right there*, but right there turned out to be a lot farther than it appeared.

All told, it took us seven hours to reach the top. Getting to the 12,400 foot summit required more than a vertical mile of climbing. Oh, and did I mention that every foot of altitude we gained made it harder and harder to breathe? Above 10,000 feet (the altitude in which WWII pilots started using oxygen), I could barely ever catch my breath. As we trudged up switchback after switchback, my heart beat a mile a minute. Our breaks became longer. The complaints of the high schoolers on our team became a constant din in the background.

The top third of the volcano was draped in a thick fog. As we walked past conifer trees and tall, wind-blown grasses, we could barely see 20 feet ahead of us. But we kept at it. Little by little we made progress. At one point, we were trudging mindlessly up yet another switchback when the scenery changed. The ground flattened out and we found ourselves looking down into the volcano's crater.

Volcán de Agua once had a lake on top (thus the name "Volcano of Water"). In 1541, an earthquake broke open the side of the crater, unleashing a torrent of water, mud, and debris onto the then colonial capital of Guatemala, Ciudad Vieja, below. I was standing right where the lake had spilled out almost 500 years before.

It took me a second to realize what this meant. *Was this it? Were we done with the climb?!?* Turns out, no. We weren't. There were still 15 minutes of climbing left to get to the actual summit. But you know what? I didn't care. We had reached the top!

Heavy fog surrounded us as we marched up the forested crater walls. When we got to the very top, however, the constantly blowing wind cleared the air. I couldn't believe my eyes. The view was clear for miles. Stretching below us in every direction was one of the most stunning panoramas I had ever seen.

It was like being in a plane. Massive cumulus formations roiled and re-shaped themselves in front of me while Volcán de Fuego and Volcán Acatenango peeked their heads through the clouds in the distance. As I looked, Volcán de Fuego, still active, shot a geyser of thick black ash into the sky. I was speechless.

A veritable forest of television, radio, and cell phone towers covered the top of Volcán de Agua, but after walking around for a bit, I found a hillside with an unobstructed view of the breath-taking sunset. I sat there for two hours, in awe of the beauty in front of me.

When the show was over, I headed back to the worker's shack where we'd be staying for the night (This is the benefit of traveling with Guatemalans. They befriended a utility worker on the way up and he let us sleep in his building instead of in a tent outside in the freezing cold).

We built a fire outside and began cooking dinner – refried beans, some questionable grilled meat, and tortillas toasted on the coals. After we ate, we spent some time in prayer and worship around the fire. Every now and then, Volcán de Fuego shot bursts of bright-hot lava into the sky. Unbelievable! Exhausted from our day's adventures, we piled up sleeping bags and blankets, and slept shoulder to shoulder like sardines in the tiny worker's shack.

The next morning, we bundled up to watch the sunrise (which was amazing),[8] packed up our gear, and headed down the mountain. One of our team had some pain in his knee, so it took us about four hours to reach the bottom. When we finally arrived in Santa Maria de Jesús, we were sweaty, covered in dust, and completely spent.

Driving back to Santo Tomás, I had a huge smile on my face. Was the trek difficult? Yes. Was it uncomfortable? Totally. Would the sausages we had for breakfast that had been in Rudi's bag uncooked for 24 hours cause me to get sick? Probably. But would I do it again in a heartbeat?

You'd better believe it!

---

[8] This sunrise is the image featured on the cover of this book.

25

Value

It was a smile I'll never forget.

My mind was whirling. I simply couldn't come to grips with what I was seeing. Beauty covering pain. Smiles covering indignity. How could these shy, giggling girls be the victims of one of history's greatest injustices?

—

During my first trip to Cambodia in 2010, I had the opportunity to interview a family in the Phnom Penh region, to sit in their home and get a glimpse into what everyday life is like for some of the poorest communities in the city. I came to their home specifically to meet a girl who would soon be part of the Daughters Project, the dress-making program of the Center for Global Impact (CGI). Her name was Sreypich.[9]

When my friend and interpreter, Aliya, and I arrived at

---

[9] I've changed all the names in this chapter to protect the family's identity.

Sreypich's home, it was early afternoon. We walked down the dirt path leading to their family's compound. Inside the fence, four small shacks sat in a line, nestled between a few shady fruit trees. The shacks, like many in Cambodia, were built on stilts to protect the house when the nearby Mekong River flooded.

Sreypich's home on the edge of Phnom Penh

Because it was the hottest part of the day, most of the family was asleep. They lay in hammocks or on mats on the floor. Only a few of the younger kids were awake, quietly playing in the dirt.

When one of them saw us, she hurried to wake up her family. Before I could get out the words, "Oh, it's OK. We can come back later!" she had begun waking everyone up. 16 year-old Sreypich came to the door, her hair messy from napping, and gave us a big smile.

Within a few minutes, Aliya and I were sitting in the middle shack talking to Sreypich's mother and aunt. Sreypich and a couple of her sisters sat on the other side of the room, whispering to each other and smiling when they heard us mention their names.

I asked the women about their lives, about their kids, and

about what life was like for them on a day-to-day basis. After quite a few clarifying questions, I was able to piece together a bit of their story. Sreypich's mother Sophoan, 40, had seven children. She made money selling eggs at a roadside kiosk. Weather permitting, her husband went fishing. In season, he was able to catch enough fish to both feed his family and make a few dollars at the market. But on windy days like the one when we visited, he always came up empty.

Sreypich's aunt Sokheak, 51, took care of five kids (the children of her other sister, who passed away several years before). With seven mouths to feed, including her 63 year-old husband's, Sokheak had a hard time making ends meet. She sold vegetables at the kiosk with her sister, but often had to rely on loans with exorbitant interest (sometimes as high as 30%) to buy food.

"It's very stressful," she told me. "I get headaches a lot."

Their story sounded similar to ones I had heard all over the world: a family struggling to make ends meet, malnourished kids too poor to finish school. The cycle of poverty personified. But as I sat and listened, I knew that there was something significantly different about this family's story. Something more sinister was happening beneath the surface, and I had a hard time coming to grips with what I knew. The truth, as explained to me a few days earlier by a staff member from CGI, is that Sreypich's family had resorted to sex trafficking to get by. Sreypich and at least two of her sisters had been sold for sex by their own mother.

I don't know what I had expected trafficking victims to look like, but Sreypich and her sisters were not it. These shy, giggling girls sitting across the room from me didn't look scarred; they weren't cowering in the corner. They were just... girls.

As we talked, I stewed over this fact in my mind. I could barely concentrate as I realized the full implications of what I was seeing. If these girls were trafficking victims, *anyone* could be. And knowing what it actually meant for these girls to have been trafficked, I had a hard time maintaining my composure.

In Cambodia, virgin girls are worth around $500, a year's wages for many impoverished families. Faced with the agonizing prospect of watching their children go hungry or the distasteful option to resort to trafficking, many parents end up choosing the latter. After negotiating a price with a "madam" (brothel manager), who takes a significant cut herself, the family of a virgin girl will send her off to be locked in a hotel room for a week. There she will be forced to have sex repeatedly by the paying man.

Once she returns home, the girl's "value" drops significantly. A non-virgin girl is worth only $30 a night. Of course, now that her dignity has been shattered, it isn't nearly as difficult for a family to send her off again. The worst part of all is that, for many girls in that community, this horrific process begins around age 12.

While it may seem abhorrent to you and me to even *think* about something like this, sex trafficking has become an accepted part of life in many impoverished communities. It is seen as simply an unpleasant act a girl must do to help provide for her family. When it happens generation after generation (girls trafficked by their mothers who were trafficked by *their* mothers and so on), the sharp sting of indignity inevitably gets pushed to the background. To think that this sort of thing happened to innocent girls absolutely broke my heart. To know that it happened simply because their parents were *poor* left me overwhelmed.

As I sat across the room from Sreypich and her sisters, I honestly didn't know how to feel. Sad? Enraged? Hopeless? Well, no. I couldn't feel hopeless. As awful as her situation was, I knew that Sreypich's life was about to change.

You see, Sreypich had just enrolled in CGI's Daughter's Project. Just a few weeks after my visit, I knew, she would move into a home with nine other girls for the year-long program. Safe, protected, and loved, Sreypich would have an opportunity to heal and to discover her true potential as she learned the valuable trade of dress-making. With a loving house mother, a beautiful garden to explore and three square meals a day, Sreypich would soon be able to rest and be herself, knowing that she would be safe.

When she finished the program, Sreypich would be a different person. She would have valuable skills. She would have confidence. Most importantly, however, she would have hope. She would know that her true value was in more than just her body. And some day, when Sreypich grew up and had a family of her own, a very different future would be in store for her children. The cycle of shame would be broken.

Sitting in that shack, my heart was a swirl of emotions. This was not a fairy-tale ending. The systems of injustice that caused so much pain would still be present in that community. Other girls would inevitably be trafficked. But I was filled with hope that the kingdom of God was on the move in at least one family. Lives were being changed, and hearts were being healed. Great things sometimes have small beginnings.

As Aliya and I walked out of the family's compound that afternoon, a single image stuck in my head. It was an image that filled me with hope: Sreypich's beautiful, bashful smile.

26

Into the Wild

Turns out camels are actually kind of nasty.

"Do you have Facebook?"

My eyes were closed. Sweaty and exhausted, the bus's air conditioning was causing me to doze off a bit.

"Do you have Facebook?" Hearing the words a second time, I opened my eyes.

Standing in front of me was a Palestinian teenager holding out a piece of paper and a pen. "I do," I said with a grin. I took the paper from him. On the page was a list of hand-written names. I added mine.

I handed the paper back to the teen. As he went up to the kids sitting in the seats in front of me, I couldn't help but smile. What I was witnessing at that moment was an unbelievably significant act.

As I watched the Dead Sea pass by on our right, I shook my head in amazement. A group of teens "friending" each other on Facebook may not seem very important. But I have never seen this common social ritual so laden with meaning.

—

As I mentioned in an earlier chapter, I had the chance to spend a month in the spring of 2011 embedded with Musalaha in the Holy Land. Their dream is to harness the transformative power of God's kingdom to bring true peace to Israel and Palestine.

One of the main ways they accomplish this mission is by making people miserable. Several times a year they take groups of Palestinian and Israeli youth, young adults, or church leaders into the desert for four days on what they call "Desert Encounters." The experience is always intense, difficult, and uncomfortable... and that's actually kind of the point.

I got to experience one of these Desert Encounters firsthand. I tagged along with a group of Messianic Jewish and Christian Palestinian teenagers and a diverse team of leaders as they hiked up mountains, rode camels and trudged through the sand in Israel's vast Negev wilderness.

The whole experience gave me a fantastic inside look at the work of Musalaha and gave me hope that their mission truly is possible.

—

The week before we left for the Negev, I had the chance to sit down with Salim J Munayer, Founder and Director of Musalaha. He talked about the mission and vision for Musalaha and gave me several insights that helped to put a lot of things into perspective as I found myself a week later leading a camel through the desert.

According to Salim, the root of the Israeli/Palestinian conflict is the dehumanization and demonization that inevitably happens when there is an imbalance of power.

By age four or five, he said, children on both sides of the conflict have developed a simple narrative to understand their world: "We are good; they are bad. We want peace; they want war." As with all generalizations, these simple ideas tend to grow into full-blown prejudice by adulthood.

Every unjust act, every crime committed, serves only to bolster these preconceptions. It's a self-reinforcing feedback loop - confirmation bias working overtime. Eventually, it becomes nearly impossible to convince a Palestinian or Israeli that their neighbors are anything other than "the enemy."

And so the conflict lingers on.

This is why the Musalaha's Desert Encounters are so brilliant. As Salim told me, "The desert is a place where the imbalance of power disappears." In the wilderness, *everyone* is sweaty and uncomfortable and tired. *Everyone* is small and helpless in the face of nature's power. In other words, everyone is human.

———

During my time with Musalaha in the desert, I got to see this concept in action. We all took turns riding and leading camels through the wilderness, but we didn't get to choose who we rode with. Palestinian and Israeli teens were put on top of the animals in pairs, forced to share (and endure!) the strange new experience not with the friends they came with, but with someone on the other side of the divide.

Hiking through a dried out riverbed, the kids helped each other climb down 15 foot high boulders. Trudging up the side of a mountain, they grumbled together about the "impossible" climb. Squeezing through a very narrow passage, the kids encouraged each other to keep moving.

Although many of the teens on the trip did not share their language, culture or history with each other, they shared a common humanity, and this is what began to break down walls.

Having finally seen all of this first-hand in the Negev, something Salim said to me during our meeting began to make more sense. At one point in our conversation, Salim had mentioned that we "cannot reverse the situation" in Israel and Palestine. "We're not here to find a solution," he said. "But I have a hope for *individuals*."

Being an idealistic guy, this struck me at the time as a little hopeless. Every problem has a solution, right? The situation has to be reversed on a large scale, doesn't it? I wondered how nation-wide reconciliation could ever happen one person at a time.

But then I spent four days in the desert with a group of teens. I watched young Israelis and Palestinians building a set of shared experiences with each other. I watched Palestinian kids listening intently to stories told by Israeli leaders. I watched Israeli adolescents goofing off with Palestinian counselors. Suddenly Salim's words didn't seem so hopeless after all.

Palestinian and Israeli students, miserable
together in the hot Negev sun

No, these teens would not go home and immediately bring an end to the Palestinian/Israeli conflict. They would not have lost all of their prejudices about each other. But the next time these kids overheard a sweeping generalization about Palestinians or Israelis, there would definitely be a bit of cognitive dissonance.

As individuals, these kids now have the potential to become advocates for one another. Knowing someone on the other side of the divide – realizing that they really aren't all that different – is the first step to true reconciliation.

But these individuals are not alone. To date, over 1000 Israeli and Palestinian teens, young adults, pastors and leaders have participated in one of Musalaha's Desert Encounters. And that number is growing all the time.

Every one of these participants is returning to his/her "normal" life with an unsettling realization that their preconceived notions need to be reconsidered; that what they have been taught about each other may not, in fact, be true.

—

As the bus drove us back to Jerusalem, I looked around at the faces of the teens who had just experienced the desert together. Some were dozing, others listening to their iPods, and a few were laughing at inside jokes from the trip.

One of them, Jonathan, was looking over the list of names he had collected: soon to be Facebook friends. The list included a Palestinian Israeli living in Jerusalem, a young Israeli man fresh out of the army, a Palestinian teenager from the West Bank, and an Israeli settlement dweller. In the hustle and bustle of city life, these young men and women would probably never have a chance to interact, their lives divided by a conflict stretching back for generations.

But after a simple shared experience in the desert, they were returning home in an unexpected way. They were returning home as friends.

27

Wrecked

No. Coke Light is NOT the same thing.

I remember the first time I got good and truly "wrecked." It was back in high school. My parents, sister, and I went on a short trip to Guinea, West Africa, where my aunt and uncle were missionaries. Being the comfort-loving picky eater that I was at the time, the whole experience was pretty rough. Fickle electricity, no air conditioning, and *no* Diet Coke. Obviously, it was a recipe for misery (and I made sure to keep letting everyone know how miserable I was).

The whole trip I was ridiculously far outside of my comfort zone. There was a mentally ill man laying on a mat outside of our guesthouse, doing odd things every time we walked by. We got absolutely covered in dust and sweat when our cross-country taxi's window wouldn't close. And then there was the massive gang of teenage girls who showed up to meet the foreigners when we stopped on the side of the road. Every one of them was topless. I was horribly embarrassed.

But of all the discomforts and "hardships" I endured, the

most difficult part was the food. We had rice with sauce for just about every meal. I know, right? Tragic. *Rice with sauce.* Looking back, I don't know why this dish struck me as so gross (maybe because it wasn't pizza?), but I simply couldn't handle it.

One day we were eating rice with some sort of peanut sauce for dinner. I could barely keep it down. I was raised better than to complain about my food, so I didn't say anything, but inside I was about to explode. "How can they expect me to eat this stuff?" I thought. "All I want is a nice, juicy hamburger. Is that too much to ask?"

Just then I looked out the window and saw an image that has been seared into my mind ever since. Right outside, standing on a small rubbish heap ten feet away, was a four-year-old child wearing nothing but a filthy t-shirt. As I watched, he reached down, picked up a banana peel from the garbage pile and started licking out the inside.

As you can imagine, I was stunned. First of all, I had never seen such an extreme demonstration of poverty before. Second, there was the fact that it happened mere *seconds* after I was griping about the giant *pile* of food on my plate. In the midst of my entitlement, a child was eating garbage to survive. The moment changed me forever.

Now, it would be foolish to say I *never* took food for granted again. Of course I did. Just days later I was whining about how there was no ice in my drink. I still had a long way to go. But the image of the child on the trash heap was one that still gives me chills whenever I think about it. It forced me to rethink my perspective on the world.

Since that day I have been "wrecked" like that countless times. Meeting a man ravaged by heroin addiction in New York City. Holding a starving baby in Port-au-Prince. Seeing 50 kids in New Delhi crammed into a school the size of my kitchen. All of these experiences have shattered my suburban worldview and have forced me to ask some difficult questions about my role in the world. They have also given me new focus and purpose when I think about how God could use me as an instrument of his kingdom.

Because of this, I believe it is *vital* for each of us to get wrecked if we ever want to fully engage with God's mission of redemption. I think it's a crucial component for every Christ-follower's faith journey. This is especially true for those of us who live in the suburbs of America, where a carefully cultivated worldview of comfort, security, and abundance keeps us blissfully unaware of the injustice around us.

Because I've placed such a high priority on "wrecking" people in the 'burbs, I've found myself increasingly intrigued by the mechanics of the process. For example, what exactly does it *mean* to get wrecked? What is going on internally? How is a person's worldview actually being affected? These questions are actually a bit harder to answer than they might initially appear.

The main reason it's so tricky, I believe, is because wrecking ball experiences like these are often processed in the midst of many *other* wild transitions. For example, when people come home from short-term trips to the developing world, they have to deal with their newfound "wreckage" in the midst of reverse culture shock, jet lag, and a changing diet. They're exhausted, constipated, *and* trying to figure out their new perspective on the world. With so many changes happening, it's sometimes hard to know exactly what is going on inside.

The same things were true of me when I first started working with the poor and marginalized. Coming home from far-flung locales, I found it difficult to tease apart the intricacies of an expanding worldview. Jet lagged at 3am and feeling like I just got hit by a train, it wasn't exactly prime time for thoughtful introspection.

But after I had been traveling for a while, something really fascinating happened. On one of my trips for World Next Door, my worldview was disrupted *without* these other external changes. I got wrecked in a test tube, so to speak. It happened during my 2010 visit to Cambodia.

By this point in my journey, I had been encountering awful injustices full-time for almost two years straight. Whether I liked it or not, I was developing some pretty thick skin. Run-of-the-mill, everyday poverty didn't have the visceral sting it used to. For example, visiting a slum community in Phnom Penh and seeing its squalid living conditions didn't paralyze me the way it once would have. I was, of course, saddened by the sight of children playing barefoot in the mud, but I had a broader context for poverty in which to understand what I was seeing. It was just another example of an injustice for which I already developed a mental category.

This was not the case, however, for the issues surrounding sex trafficking. I had not encountered them before, so I was in for quite a shock when I learned what was going on. For instance, there was Sophoan, the mother who had sold her daughter Sreypich for sex to help put food on the table. At Rapha House I had met a *six-year-old girl* who had been recently rescued from a brothel. I got to know many teenage girls who were constantly at risk of being lured away by conmen and tricked into a life of sex slavery.

As I learned about the plight of these girls and heard story after story that made my stomach turn, I got *good* and wrecked. I went from outrage to bitterness to helplessness and back again. I watched my old perspective of the world fall to pieces and a new one take its place. But as my heart was going through all of this turmoil, my body and mind were just fine. I wasn't jet-lagged, sick, or culture-shocked. It all just happened in my heart. And this is where I came to understand just what is happening when a person like me gets wrecked.

We all have categories that make up our worldview. Little pieces of the pie that, when added together, make up the entirety of the way we see the world: this is what a family looks like, this is what it means to have plenty, this is what I'm entitled to, this is what a home feels like, this is what it means to follow Jesus, and so on.

When we get wrecked, however, a *new* category arises that doesn't fit into the pie. When I saw that toddler eating a banana peel from my uncle's trash heap, the concept didn't fit anywhere in my existing categories. My understanding of home, food, provision… none of these could capture what I was seeing. And so, a new category was forcefully wedged into the pie, causing the long, slow process of reshaping my view of the world.

The same thing happened to me in Cambodia. A six-year-old girl rescued from a brothel? That didn't fit anywhere in my worldview. A mother selling her own daughter for sex? What am I supposed to do with that? As I learned about the horrific realities of sex trafficking, a new category was added to my mind and I have not been the same ever since.

Even though I wasn't shocked at American culture when I returned home or completely destroyed by a changing diet, I did have to re-enter "life as usual" with a new category added to my worldview - a new way of understanding just how broken humanity really is. Jet lag was getting easier to deal with, but there was no shortcut for rebuilding after a wrecking ball experience. However, as painful and inconvenient as it was, I started to understand how vital getting wrecked was for my development and how big a role it played in shaping my calling. These days I believe this is true for all of us. Having our worldview destroyed and rebuilt is the first step in becoming who God wants us to be.

My dad often talks about Christ-followers suffering from a never-ending "low-grade fever of sadness." When we truly understand how the world is broken, we can still go on with our daily lives. Just like being sick with a low-grade fever we can work and laugh and play. But underneath it all is an understanding that we will not be whole until the kingdom of God comes in all its fullness. It is this awareness, this "low grade fever" that gives us a reason to have hope - a reason to dedicate our lives to the kingdom's coming.

We don't choose to fight for hope and justice in the world because we saw it on a list of commands somewhere. We do it because we know that we will never be whole and satisfied until the kingdom is here.

My chosen profession for the last six years has exposed me to more wrecking balls than most. I won't lie and say it's been easy. My heart breaks often for the suffering and pain of the world. But now, more than ever, I am filled with a passionate and fervent hope that Christ's kingdom is expanding in this world. I am fired up to give every moment of my life to that end. Because I've been wrecked so many times, I can pray to God with more conviction than ever before, "Your kingdom come, your will be done, on earth as it is in heaven."

28

The Greenhouse

---

*The green pepper was the
size of a basketball.*

As I've traveled the world for the last few years, I've come
to realize a pretty grim truth. There are *no* quick fixes for
poverty. There are no "magic bullets" that can reverse an
insurmountable network of injustices in one fell swoop. They
just don't exist.

But hey. It's worth a shot, right!? (He says sarcastically)

—

I first visited Huruma Slum in 2009, before World Next
Door had even officially begun. The community is tucked away
in the green and wooded northern edge of Nairobi. Huruma's
residents used to work on nearby farms, but they lost their jobs
when much of the area's land was purchased by wealthy
politicians and expats looking to build massive homes on
sweeping country estates. Today, the area is home to some of
the richest inhabitants of Nairobi, and the residents in Huruma

have no choice but to work for them as guards, gardeners, and maids.

Although the slum is nestled on the side of a beautiful, green valley, it maintains many of the problems of its urban counterparts. Sanitation is poor, food is scarce, there is a lack of clean water, and many children are unable to receive an adequate education.

One of the main issues Huruma faces regarding food is its location, smack in the middle of a wealthy suburb. The only place nearby to buy fresh fruits and vegetables is in the middle of a very expensive shopping mall. I've been to that mall's greengrocer (a.k.a. produce market) a few times, and even I, as an American, was shocked at the prices.

For people in the slum to buy food they could actually afford, they'd need to take public transportation into Nairobi or far out into rural Kenya, a time consuming and expensive proposition, not a real possibility for people with such little money. So even with a big produce market nearby, people in Huruma struggled to put food on the table, and malnourished children were commonplace.

On one of my visits to Huruma, I encountered a non-profit organization which had decided to address this problem head-on. Through the generosity of Western donors, they had built a large greenhouse to grow fresh fruits and vegetables. The idea seemed flawless. They'd provide jobs for people in the slum while selling fresh produce to its residents, making the project financially sustainable in the process. Brilliant!

At least, it looked that way on the surface.

When I took a tour of the greenhouse, I was very impressed. The whole operation was orderly, well-kept, and clean. The workers I met were happy and seemed to take real satisfaction in their work. On top of everything, the vegetables they were growing were absolutely *incredible*. Walking down one row of beautiful greenery, my jaw dropped as I looked at the largest green peppers I had ever seen.

There was only one small problem. The produce they were growing was *too* good. Growing such high-quality vegetables from such top-shelf seeds was not cheap. People in Huruma couldn't afford to pay what it would cost for this project to become financially self-sufficient. So the non-profit needed to find a different market for their goods. The only real option was to sell their vegetables to the greengrocer at the nearby shopping mall.

In the end, tens of thousands of dollars were invested in this project, but the people of Huruma got nothing more than a handful of new jobs. That was it.

It may be a bit of an extreme example, but to me, this greenhouse is a perfect representation of how *not* to bring aid to suffering people. It was a "magic bullet," an ideal solution solving multiple problems in one fell swoop. On paper, it looked phenomenal. In reality, it was a wash.

Yet again, I'm convinced the *only* way to bring about long-term, sustainable change in impoverished communities is by partnering with indigenous leaders, allowing *them* to create new projects and solutions, and supporting the local Church as it brings healing to its community.

Americans like me may have amazing ideas, but our innovations count for little next to the deep, lasting change made possible by those who are in it for the long haul.

29

Penelakut

I feel like smoke inhalation is becoming a theme in my life.

My eyes burned. Thick wood smoke from two roaring fires assaulted my lungs and eyes. I knew I'd smell like a campfire for weeks. In front of me, Penelakut dancers in full ceremonial garb spun and danced to the beat of drums. My first experience in a First Nations Big House was well underway, and I had a look of sheer incredulity on my face.

How in the world did I end up here?!?

—

It was my first day on Penelakut Island in British Columbia. I had come to the Pacific Northwest to write about the work of ROOTS, a program focused on helping Native American youth reconnect with the Creator through outdoor activities like archery, kayaking, fishing, and camping.

In the morning, the leaders of my host ministry, Tal James and Tim Christensen, had given me a tour of Penelakut. Then they decided to throw me in head first. Just as we were getting ready to leave the island, Tim turned to me and said, "Do you want to go up to the Big House tonight?"

"Uh, sure. Yeah. I'm up for anything." I replied, not knowing exactly what he was talking about.

"OK, then here are the keys to my truck. Just make sure to catch the 8pm ferry and I'll see you at my house later tonight. See ya!"

"Uh, OK then..." I said, hoping I'd remember how to get back.

Tim and Tal hopped in another vehicle and drove away. Apparently I was on my own. I turned back to Tal's parents' house to find my guide for the evening, Tal's brother John.

The Big House. Hmmm... This will be an interesting experience, I thought as I opened the door. There was only one *tiny* question I needed to have answered. "Tell me again. What exactly *is* the Big House?"

Like most of my crazy World Next Door experiences, I figured it would all become clear in time.

———

A few weeks before that night, as I was preparing to live and work on a First Nations reservation for the first time, I compiled a mental checklist of what I knew about the people I'd be visiting.

"Let's see. They lived in teepees. They used to fight cowboys. Hmmm. They were in tune with nature? They live on reservations now?"

Uh oh. This was not the voluminous database of knowledge I was hoping for.

My trip to British Columbia was drawing near and all I could conjure up about the people I'd be working with was the stuff I learned through my first grade social studies class (and having Dances with Wolves in my Netflix queue, of course). My understanding of Native Americans was about as nuanced as a playground game of Cowboys and Indians.

I had a lot to learn.

So I studied up. I read a stack of books about the history

and culture of the people I'd be visiting. What I learned honestly blew my mind.

One thing I picked up right off the bat is that "Native Americans" prefer the term "First Nations" in Canada. This makes sense when you think about it. How would you like having your people named after Amerigo Vespucci, the cartographer whose people killed and enslaved your ancestors?

Another thing I learned is that First Nations people *still exist*. It seems obvious, but in my home town of Indianapolis, where there are relatively few indigenous people alive today, it's easy to think of First Nations people as little more than a footnote in our history textbooks. But in the Pacific Northwest, their communities are alive and well.

Finally, I learned that First Nations folks today are in the middle of a protracted struggle to regain the land and rights they have lost. Although the 1850s may seem like ancient history to us in the suburbs of America, the conflicts from that time continue to impact legislation and culture today.

It all began with a clash of cultures. In the 1800's, colonizers on the Northwest Coast began to view First Nations culture as barbaric. They interpreted their religious ceremonies as evil. They thought that hunting and gathering (instead of farming) was a sign of backwardness.

And let's face it. To a European civilization trying to expand and exploit the abundant natural resources of the land, these "uneducated Indians" were simply in the way. First Nations people put up a fight when their land was taken away, they got in skirmishes with white farmers over traditional hunting grounds and they protested the destruction of their land through logging and mining. Not exactly a conducive environment for rapid colonial expansion.

So, in an attempt "to solve the Indian problem," the Canadian government decided to partner with the Christian Church to assimilate and "civilize" aboriginal people. Their solution was to create a system of compulsory residential schools that would take First Nations children out of their homes and educate them in the knowledge and culture of the "civilized" world. If these kids were taught English and converted to Christianity, it was thought, they would no longer be a problem.

Starting in the mid-1800s, the government divided Canada up among the country's major Christian denominations (Catholic, Anglican, United, and Methodist) and started building the schools.

Put simply, the schools were terrible places. Children, some as young as three, were taken from their families and forced to live in horrific conditions: inadequate healthcare, inedible food, and many, many cases of physical, emotional, spiritual, and sexual abuse. Each child was given a "Christian Name" (e.g. Norman, Elsie, Clara, John, etc.) and was punished for speaking his/her native tongue. The more I learned about these Residential Schools, the more my heart broke at the truly nauseating and despicable things that were done to them there.

This hillside on Penelakut Island was once the site of an infamous Residential School.

I learned that the real legacy of these terrible schools was not just the individual acts of abuse and exploitation that happened to kids who attended, as awful as those were. The schools' legacy also extended deep into the lives of the survivors' children and grandchildren.

Residential school survivors entered into adulthood without having ever lived in a healthy family environment. They had no idea what it meant to be a parent. They had never been taught adequate problem solving skills and had no idea how to pass on traditional values to their children.

On top of it all, these survivors had grown up to become parents who had never dealt with the deep emotional scars of abuse. As a result, unemployment was normal. Alcoholism was rampant. Suicide was frequent.

Having such brokenness infused into a society would be bad enough if it happened to one generation. But imagine if it happened to the next one. And the next. And the next.

Even though most residential schools closed their doors by the end of the 1970's, the survivors and their families were set on a multi-generational spiral of injustice that continued to wind ever downward. Suddenly, my trip to Penelakut Island carried undertones far deeper and more significant than I had ever imagined before. I left for British Columbia with eyes wide open to the systemic injustice still bearing consequences today.

———

About an hour after Tim and Tal left, John and I drove up to the Big House and parked outside. The sky was darkening as we headed to the door. The Big House on Penelakut Island was a giant wooden building modeled after the community longhouses that were the standard living and meeting places for the Penelakut before the arrival of Europeans.

Each winter, the Big House became a bustle of activity for the community as they celebrated night after night of traditional winter dances. This was what I had the privilege of witnessing that evening.

As we walked into the building, all I could see was smoke. Two giant fires burned in the center of the long dirt floor, casting up peals of dark, rich smoke into the room. There were two big holes cut into the roof to act as vents, but it became clear immediately that the majority of the smoke was going straight into my eyes, into my lungs, and deep into every fiber of my clothing.

Eyes stinging, I took a look around. Through the smoke, I could see initiate dancers preparing for the night's events. Being the stupid American that I was, I immediately went up and introduced myself to one of them. She didn't respond.

"Um, we're not really allowed to talk to them while they're in training," John told me.

Nice. My first act in the Big House was to make a major fool of myself.

I apologized, laughing at my idiocy, and grabbed a seat to observe the night's events.

Now, here is where things get tricky. You see, the dances I witnessed were full of amazing and thought-provoking moments. As a writer, there are many things I could share to help you get a picture of what was happening inside.

But the events inside the Big House were very private to the Penelakut. The dances were intensely personal, emotional, and spiritual for the people involved. It was an unbelievable privilege for me to even *be* there. Because of that, and because I want to do everything I can to respect the folks I met, I have to keep the details of what I saw in the Big House to myself.

That said, I can still tell you what I *learned*.

The Penelakut winter dances were a fascinating mix of tradition, spirituality, artistic expression, and entertainment. In the days before European settlement, the dances were performed after the fall hunting and gathering seasons came to an end. The community lived together in the Big House to ride out the cold winter months and to welcome neighboring tribes and communities for celebrations.

The unique songs and dances performed around the fires were passed down from generation to generation to worship the Creator, tell stories from the past, and remind everyone of their connection to their ancestors and the earth.

The dances served as a broad illustration for me of what was happening among the Penelakut people, and I thought about this a lot as I watched the dancers perform. As their nation continued to grow and develop, the Penelakut faced the influx of modern Western culture daily. How would they maintain the traditions of the past when they had to compete with Xboxes, reality TV, and Facebook? More significantly, how would they undo the loss of pride and dignity that came from a century of enslavement and exploitation?

Many traditions had been nearly forgotten. Others had been lost entirely. But the Penelakut I met had not given up. Despite the damage that had been done, they were eager to reclaim the traditions that gave them their national identity. The winter dances were one such way they could remain connected to their past.

Thankfully, they were not alone in this struggle. My hosts Tim and Tal, leaders of ROOTS, were wholeheartedly dedicated to the people of Penelakut. Tal, in fact, *was* Penelakut. He was born and raised on the island.

As followers of Christ, they were both eager to heal the wounds of the past by helping Penelakut youth reconnect with the knowledge and prowess of their ancestors (the acronym "ROOTS" actually stands for "Reclaiming Original Outdoor Technology and Skills"). Rather than coming in with an agenda to "fix" the people of Penelakut, they were focused on drawing out the knowledge, pride, and traditions that were already there.

After the things I had learned about First Nations history by this point, this struck me as a great perspective. With a long history of outsiders coming in to say, "You have to be someone else," it was remarkably refreshing to see a ministry that says, "Be who you are."

I got to watch Tal and Tim work tirelessly with the leaders and elders of the community to provide engaging and dignifying experiences for young people on the island. By taking kids on "survival" camping trips, Tal and Tim proved to the kids they were capable of something they never thought they could do before. Through awesome archery and kayaking experiences, the kids found self-confidence and learned the joys of being out in nature.

And this, to me, is the most significant thing. Tim, a trained and experienced cross-cultural veteran, could leverage his skills and gifts to support Penelakut leaders. Tal, a skilled and talented servant in his own right, was a walking testimony of the transformative power of the Creator among his own people.

A young Penelakut man practices archery with Tim after school

It's been said that the roots of the past bear fruit in the present. On Penelakut Island, the roots of a broken past continue to bear fruit of brokenness today. But Tal and Tim have dedicated their lives to *replacing* these broken roots with roots of hope and healing. And they base it all in the love of Christ.

—

As I left the Big House that night, I reeked of woodsmoke and my mind was running a million miles an minute. Driving Tim's truck down to the 8pm ferry, I couldn't shake the big, silly grin plastered all over my face.

I had come to Penelakut expecting to find only brokenness, despair, and hopelessness. Instead, I had found the seedlings of a community reborn. I had witnessed the pride of a people no longer ashamed of their true identities. And I had seen the kingdom of God being lived out through two men whose message to the people of Penelakut was simple:

"The Creator loves you. We love you. And you have so much to offer the world."

30

River Babies

I tried the analogy with puppies. It just doesn't pack the same punch.

Every summer throughout the life of World Next Door we led two-month internships to different countries around the world. Three to five young writers would join our team and write articles for our blog and digital magazine. While they were there, our interns lived in host homes, worked with a local ministry, and told stories of hope to their readers back home. It was awesome.

I had a blast leading these interns, especially because I got to teach them some of the things I was learning through my *own* travels. Over time, I got pretty adamant about some of my policies:

"You're there to learn, not to do!"

"Always end your articles in hope!"

"Have a palms-up approach!"

The interns would tease me because I sometimes sounded

like a broken record, but I kept at it, because these were philosophies I felt *really* strongly about.

However, of all the things I taught my team each year, one lesson stood out as the most useful and thought-provoking of them all. It was a simple allegory that helped us each identify our roles for the summer. I had adapted and expanded it from something I'd heard somewhere else, but it quickly became a foundational part of World Next Door's internal language.

The allegory goes something like this:

———

Imagine you live in a village deep in the jungle. Life is simple and peaceful for you. Nothing very exciting ever really happens. One day, however, while you and some of your friends head out to go hunting, everything changes. As you walk, you come up to a river. One of your friends points and says, "Hey! Look. There's something floating in the water."

You all look where he's pointing and see a woven basket drifting down the swift current. Inside, you can hear a sound. You strain your ears to listen over the rushing water. That's when you realize what the sound is. It's a baby crying! There is a baby in that basket, just drifting down the river. That's when it dawns on you. There is a waterfall just a bit farther downstream. If nobody pulls the basket out of the river, the baby will go off the edge and surely die!

Immediately, you and your friends jump into action. A couple of you dive into the river, swim out to intercept the basket, and pull it back to shore. The others help pull you back onto dry land. Someone opens the basket, and sure enough, there is a tiny little baby inside.

"I can't believe that just happened," says one of your friends.

"It's a good thing we got here when we did," says another.

As she is saying this, another crying sound hits your ears. Everyone looks at the baby in the basket, but it's not him. You look up with dismay to see *another* basket in the river. Inside is *a different* baby. You and your friends exchange glances and prepare to jump back into the river. Just then, you notice the second basket is not alone. Behind it floats another. And then another. Within moments, the entire river is covered with baskets, each one with a fragile life inside. Hundreds and hundreds of babies, floating helplessly to the waterfall.

At this point, you have a decision to make. There are far too many babies for you to possibly save alone. Even if you and your friends did everything you possibly could to help, you would barely make a dent in the problem. How are you going to respond? What are you going to do?

There are essentially four options in front of you.

You could become a **leaver**, throwing up your hands in resignation and walking away, saying "There's no way I can stop this problem. It's not even worth trying!"

You could become a **jumper**, diving into the river again and again, saving as many individual babies as possible until all of your energy is spent. Sure, you're not going to fix the problem, but you *will* save at least a few precious lives.

You could become a **seeker**, leaving the banks of the river and heading upstream. Perhaps by searching intently you can find and *stop* whoever is throwing these babies into the river in the first place.

Finally, you could become a **shouter**, running back to the village as fast as you can to raise the alarm and spread the word, "There are babies in the river! We need more people to help!!!"

What role will you choose to play?

—

It doesn't take a rocket scientist to figure out what the allegory represents. The injustice in our world - poverty, hunger, sex trafficking, disease, war - it's an overwhelming river of need. People are suffering and dying every day, all over the world, and the problem is infinitely greater than any individual could ever possibly address. There are countless babies in the river, and we each have a choice to make.

Will we be **leavers**? Will we give up before we even start because of the magnitude of injustice? It seems like an inconceivable option, and yet many choose to take it. When faced with the AIDS pandemic or the caste system or genocide, the natural question to ask is, "What could I possibly do?" We wash our hands of the problem and walk away.

If we *do* choose to act, there are plenty of options for how to get involved. We can be **jumpers**, diving in and helping as many individuals as possible. These are the clinic workers, the teachers, the caretakers, the orphanage directors, the counselors, the adoptive parents, etc. And this is a crucial role in our struggle against injustice. We need brave people to step up and *spend themselves* on behalf of the poor and marginalized.

But simply rescuing individuals will never be enough. We also need **seekers**, willing to find and attack the root *causes* of injustice. These are the lawyers working to prosecute sex traffickers, the advocates seeking education reform, the activists standing up against the caste system, the developers working on agricultural sustainability, the investigators exposing corruption, etc. We have to do whatever we can to pull up injustice by the roots and attack it at its source.

Finally, we need **shouters**. These are people like me, focused intently on getting *more* people down to the river to serve. We learn about the needs, see what God is doing, then tell those stories to anyone who will listen. These are the journalists, the storytellers, the artists, the musicians, the preachers, the writers, the photographers, etc. We won't rest until everyone is doing their part.

Each of these roles is crucial in combatting the injustice of our world and none of them can stand alone. If we truly want to see the kingdom of God spread into the dark and broken corners of our planet, we each need to find our place in God's mission and give ourselves to it with everything we've got. God will give us the strength to carry on. He'll guide our steps and surround us with like-minded followers of Christ. All we have to do is *act*.

Doing nothing is not an option.

31

More Than a School

I guess Ukrainian folk dancing hasn't made it to rural Guatemala yet.

We were halfway to the top of Volcán de Agua. My traveling companions and I were starting to feel the altitude take its toll. The group, made up of mostly high school students, stopped at a bend in the path to catch our breath. We threw down our packs and made ourselves as comfortable as we could, massaging sore muscles and taking sips of water from our bottles. Without saying a word, the young men naturally formed a circle around Rudi, the eldest member of our group.

Although I couldn't understand much of what was being said (my Spanish hadn't improved much since high school), it was clear the boys deeply respected Rudi. As he spoke of his faith and of his relationship with God, they were hanging on every word.

Out of nowhere, I was struck with an image of Jesus and

his disciples. There may not have been many volcanoes in ancient Israel, but this image – a group of men taking a breather on the side of the road, the young disciples listening with rapt attention to their leader's words – would have been commonplace in the space between the verses we read in the gospels.

It was a beautiful moment, and one I'll undoubtedly remember the next time I read about the life of Jesus. But there was something a little surprising about this scene. Rudi, the man these kids were learning from, wasn't their pastor. He wasn't their church small group leader. No. Rudi was their high school principal.

Huh?!? The absurdity of that statement gets me every time. How many of your past school principals evoke images of Jesus with his disciples?

It was an odd juxtaposition of roles, but this was only one of many moments during my time in Guatemala that left me scratching my head about what I was seeing. Saber y Gracia (Wisdom and Grace) Christian School wasn't some run of the mill educational institution. Something was very different there.

But what was it? What made this school so different that its principal took on the role of a rabbi and nobody batted an eye? This was the question I set out to answer during my month in the village of Santo Tomás Milpas Altas in the highlands of central Guatemala.

———

When I first arrived at Saber y Gracia (SyG), I didn't know exactly what to do with myself. My Spanish was poor, the students had no idea who I was, and it was far too early to start writing anything about the school. So I just hung out and wandered around the property, meeting students during their free time.

I quickly discovered how much the kids loved looking through my pictures. The entire first week was filled with shouts of "Photo! Photo!" whenever the recess bell rang (it took them another week to learn my actual name). I'd grab my iPad, sit down on a low cement wall and flip through photos from Kenya, Haiti, India, Ukraine, Cambodia, etc. while a giant mass of red-uniform-wearing students pressed in from every side to get a glimpse.

During one of these photo-sharing sessions, I flipped through shots of my visit to Rome when one of the students grabbed my arm and asked me to back up. José, a 10th grader, wanted to see the photo of Trevi Fountain again. I went back to that photo and he began gesturing excitedly and talking about something.

In my broken understanding of Spanish I heard, "Something something horses something god something water something horses." I was lost. Did he just really love horses or something? Was he excited that someone once carved a horse out of marble?

No. As it turns out, José was absolutely fascinated by Greek mythology. Although he had never seen Trevi Fountain before, he immediately recognized Poseidon, the god of the sea, and his team of winged horses. As we spoke more (through an interpreter), it was clear José had a hunger for knowledge about history and mythology and would gobble up any resources on the subject he could get his hands on. I would not be surprised if José became an archaeologist one day.

To be totally honest, I was quite taken aback by José's eagerness to learn. I'd met countless kids in many developing countries, and it was a rare thing to find one whose worldview expanded beyond their own little slice of the globe.

It didn't take me long, however, to realize José wasn't the only kid like this at Saber y Gracia. In fact, over my four weeks with the school, I met many who had visions of a future far grander than I would have ever expected.

One student I met wanted to become an architect. Another wanted to study accounting in college so she could open a restaurant. I even met a sixth grader who wanted to become a systems engineer when he grew up. What kind of sixth grader knows what a systems engineer even is?!?

I was blown away. Here was a school in a poverty-stricken

community, attended by the children of farmers and manual laborers, yet full to the brim with dreamers, with learners, with visionaries.

I want to reiterate how crazy this is. The vast majority of young people in the poor communities I've visited around the world do not have a vision for their lives beyond what their parents and their parents' parents have done. Yes, a few might beat the odds and break away, but it is absolutely *normal* for kids in communities like this to drop out of school early, get low-paying jobs, and watch as the cycle of poverty continues its endless spiral in their lives. But not at Saber y Gracia. Something was different there. These kids had *dreams*. What in the world was going on?

Saber y Gracia teacher Lauren Pupchik and principal Rudi Pineda, holding the season's first lettuce harvest from Rudi's farm

I began to get my answer one morning when Rudi Pineda, the school's principal (and now a dear friend of mine), gave me a tour of some of the classrooms. We looked in on several different age levels while he described to me their philosophy of education.

It started all the way back in kindergarten, he explained, as we walked into a classroom full of adorable little ones. Saber y

Gracia put a lot of emphasis on critical thinking, instead of just rote memorization. While most schools in the area had their kindergarteners mindlessly learning the letters of the alphabet, SyG's students were taught actual comprehension.

He pointed to the alphabet on the wall and described how they took things slowly, helping the kids understand how each letter is used and how they interact (Q and U get married, of course!).

It took time. And this had actually caused some conflicts with several parents at the school. Rudi told me they would come into his office and confront him, complaining, "This other school's kindergarteners are already on the letter 'S.' Our child is lagging behind!" Rudi would graciously listen to their frustrations, then explain (I'm paraphrasing here), "Yes, but most of the students from *that* school fail their college entrance exams. Far more of Saber y Gracia's students pass because they've learned to think for themselves."

As he explained this to me, I couldn't help but think back to my own education. Reading comprehension and critical thinking were at the very core of how I learned. And that was in a public school. I don't think I've ever fully appreciated just what a solid education I received. This type of learning simply wasn't the norm in rural Guatemala.

We continued our tour, looking in on several different age levels. In one of the classes, we met a high school senior named Ángel who had been assigned to the school by a social worker. He told us, "I know God had a plan in it, because if it wasn't for this school, I'd be lost." What did Ángel want to become after college? An *auditor*. Again, what?!?

These kids were receiving a world-class education. Critical thinking and a focus on comprehension made Saber y Gracia's students unique. But I knew that couldn't be all. A solid philosophy of education isn't enough to explain why the students I met had such boundless confidence in their own potential. I knew there had to be something more. And guess what? There was.

—

Every Monday morning at Saber y Gracia, the students crowded into their multipurpose meeting hall (really just four adjacent classrooms with their walls removed) for chapel: a time of singing, prayer, and teaching. The music was loud, the kids were packed in like sardines, and everybody had a blast. Chapel happened every week while school was in session, and I got to sit in on it four times. The highlight of each always ended up being Rudi's message to the students.

Every week he cast a vision for the kids about what they could be. He drove home the idea that they were each children of God and that they could become anything they wanted if they worked hard enough. Normally, this "reach for your dreams" message would have struck me as cheesy and saccharine. As a suburban American, the phrase "you can be anything you want to be" had become cliché. But in those Monday morning chapel sessions, it struck me as completely relevant and down to earth for where these kids were.

Here's why. As I was preparing some "next steps" for the magazine issue I was working on, I gave several Saber y Gracia students the chance to share any prayer requests they might have. I expected lots of, "That I do well on exams," or "That my family's crops grow well this year." Imagine my surprise, then, when almost every single student jumped immediately into describing his or her broken family.

"My father has left us and is living with another family now."

"My dad is unfaithful to my mom."

"My parents are divorced."

"My dad ignores us on the street."

It was the same story over and over and over again. Student after student faced the chaos of a broken family, the emptiness of an absentee father, and the heartbreak of shattered promises.

In conversations with Rudi and Lauren (an American missionary who teaches at the school), it became quickly apparent that these were not special cases. The difficulties these young men and women faced were all too common in

Santo Tomás. That's why Rudi's "reach for your dreams" message seemed so utterly relevant in chapel.

You see, these students needed someone to believe in them. They needed someone to draw out their passions and gifts and dreams. And that's exactly what Rudi was doing. In a community plagued by absentee dads, Rudi was taking on the role of a father, offering encouragement, love, and advice.

During one chapel session, for example, Rudi spoke passionately to the adolescent girls in attendance. He explained that boys who wanted to sleep with them didn't respect them and that they should wait to have sex until they were married. Again, old news for someone like me who grew up in the American Evangelical Church, but these are kids who hadn't had "the talk" with their parents, who hadn't been told they had value, that they were worth it.

Two young men attending Saber y Gracia

Sitting in that crowded room week after week, I was in awe of the paternal care Rudi took in leading these kids. And that awe only grew when I realized his team of teachers took the same posture. These educators were involved in their students' lives. They took an active interest in their emotional development. They were, quite simply, *parents* to their students.

This was so much more than just a school. With critical thinking, paternal care, and love evident everywhere I looked, it was obvious Saber y Gracia was a school set apart from the rest. Something was different there. It was one-of-a-kind. But there was one more thing that made Saber y Gracia phenomenal: everything, *everything* they did was infused with Christ.

This was significant. Although Guatemala was highly "Christian," the vast majority of Guatemalans were Catholic. Their "faith" was often composed of rituals, icons, and strict traditions. It was not uncommon to find people who believed if they participated in an Easter parade, they were somehow earning the forgiveness of their sins.

Saber y Gracia, on the other hand, was focused on *faith*, and their leaders constantly encouraged students to have a personal relationship with Jesus. Worship songs and Bible lessons were just the beginning. Classes routinely brought in biblical themes, teachers often shared their own faith journeys with students, and prayer was completely common at the school. Never was this more apparent than at Campamento, the annual Saber y Gracia high school camp.

Campamento was one part summer camp, one part youth-group retreat, one part prom. The weekend was a three-day firehose of games, worship services, and small group sessions. It was easily the highlight of the year for the high school students at Saber y Gracia, and I got the chance to participate.

I won't get into all the details of what went on, but suffice it to say, I got to see a whole different side of Saber y Gracia. The kids were unleashed to worship like crazy. Without grade-school students around, the teaching got even more deep and personal. The Holy Spirit was moving powerfully. At one point, I even got to play a part in one student's experience.

—

The worship band had just kicked off a new song, the brass section blaring their instruments full blast. All the kids screamed with glee when they recognized the tune and started clustering into raucous dance parties around the room.

I shot some video for a couple of minutes, then put down my camera and joined in the fun. I latched on to the end of a conga line, soon finding myself in a circle of jumping, dancing, laughing teenage boys. As we shouted the lyrics to "El Señor es Mi Rey" ("the Lord is my King"), I thought I'd start a dance-off. I dropped into a squat position and started kicking my legs out in the traditional Ukrainian "Hopak" dance. They all looked at me like I was nuts. Whatever. It was fun.

After worship, we all collapsed sweaty and tired into our seats. Rudi spoke for a few minutes about the difference between religion and true faith. The kids listened attentively to his passion and conviction. Then Rudi gave the students a chance to respond. Even though they normally didn't do this until the third day of camp, Rudi asked if any students wanted to give their lives to Christ right then and there.

More than 40 students went forward immediately. They gathered in a crowd in front of the stage while Rudi began praying over them. I joined the other teachers in a circle around the outside of the students with our hands outstretched in a posture of blessing.

As we prayed, I saw one young man weeping openly in the crowd. Great sobs shook his body. Looking at him, I felt a clear nudge from the Holy Spirit to go over and give him a hug. "He needs to feel the Father's embrace," the Spirit seemed to say. "Go represent Him to this young man."

I hesitated. *Aw, but there are like 3 teachers closer to him*, I thought. *I don't speak much Spanish. It would be awkward, right?*

No answer. Just another nudge.

Alright, fine! I said in my head as I started working my way through the crowd.

When I reached the sobbing young man, I put my arms around him and pulled him into a bear hug, wondering just how awkward things were about to get for us. Immediately he turned towards me, buried his head into my shoulder, and wept for 15 minutes straight. To my surprise, the whole experience wasn't awkward at all. In fact, it was immediately apparent that the hug was exactly what he needed at that moment.

As we stood there, surrounded by other weeping, embracing, praying students, I thought about how many of them came from broken homes with abusive and absentee fathers. I realized how significant it was for one of them to come face-to-face with God the Father.

All of a sudden, I was struck with just how crazy the whole situation was. This was a school. This wasn't a church. This wasn't a youth group. This was a *school*. In that moment, surrounded by weeping, broken, transformed, hopeful young people, the threads came together.

Saber y Gracia was providing their students with an education better than anything else around. Its teachers were giving the kids the paternal and maternal love they were so often missing at home. And in a ritualistic religious culture, they were representing life-changing faith to their students.

I had figured it out. Saber y Gracia was so much more than just a school - because it was a *ministry*.

As I came to this conclusion, I realized something else: this ministry needed to grow. Reaching 264 students with this high-quality education, this paternal love, and this Christ-focused message wasn't enough. Saber y Gracia should have been reaching 500 students. Or even 1000. This ministry needed to grow.

Thankfully, I wasn't the only one who felt that way. God had been putting this burden on Rudi's heart as well. One afternoon, I joined him for a walk through his farm. The property had belonged to his family for many years, and it was the proceeds from that land's crops that sustained Saber y Gracia in the early years.

On this day, however, Rudi was interested in planting a different kind of seed on this fertile ground. As we walked between rows of freshly planted lettuce, he painted a picture of what God had laid on his heart: a new school building on his family's land, large enough to educate 1000 students, centrally located to be a hub of education for underprivileged kids from surrounding villages as well.

Hearing Rudi talk about his vision for the new school, it

was clear this wasn't about fame or numbers or influence. Shoot. If he had wanted any of those things, he would have quit a long time before! No. I am absolutely convinced this was about one thing and one thing only: changing lives.

You see, Rudi's vision wasn't to educate kids. It wasn't even to break the cycle of poverty in their lives. It was much bigger than that. His vision was to transform his entire community for the kingdom of God. He wanted to be God's instrument to bring healing to families, hope to the hopeless, and life where once there was only death.

Under normal circumstances, a school principal discipling students on the side of a volcano might have seemed odd. But after spending a month in rural Guatemala, it made perfect sense to me. Why? Because Saber y Gracia was so much more than just a school.

32

Rain

It felt like my contacts were made out of sand.

A few years ago, my dad and I went to see a movie. When we arrived, it was a beautiful sunny day. But when we walked out of the theater, it was pouring rain. Heavy, massive rain drops pounded the sidewalk and a veritable *river* stood between us and our cars. Of course, neither of us had brought an umbrella, so we were forced to wait. We watched from inside the theater as the water just fell and fell. Eventually, the downpour began to let up slightly, so we gave in and ran out to our cars, getting soaked in the process.

At the time, all I could think about was how big a hassle the rain was. I didn't want to run to my car. I didn't want to leap over massive puddles. I didn't want to get wet. But later that summer, after living in Kibera Slum for a month, my perspective on rain began to change.

It had been a very dry couple of months in Kenya. I heard

many people say that it was the driest it had been in years. In June and July, the months immediately following Kenya's rainy season, it had only rained twice.

I was able to see the effects of this drought firsthand on the property of Tumaini Church, the host ministry where I spent my days. When I first arrived, the red dirt was packed down and the air was clear. Over several weeks, however, the tightly packed dirt began to slowly break apart into a fine layer of rust-colored dust. Under the bright sun, this dust layer grew and grew until it was almost an *inch* thick.

With so much dust on the ground, simply walking from place to place kicked up enough of it to make the legs of my jeans red. When kids ran around playing, entire clouds of dust would hang in the air. One girl with a jumprope was completely shrouded in a red haze as she bounced.

I could *feel* the change too. In my lungs. In my eyes. I started coughing a lot more. Sneezing. Taking my contacts out each night became a highly anticipated ritual of relief. I found myself checking the sky several times a day, wishing for even a gentle shower to pack the dust back into the ground where it belonged.

But as much as it irritated my eyes and lungs, the drought carried with it far more debilitating implications for my neighbors in the slum. First of all, Kenya's electricity grid was overwhelmingly dependent on hydro-electric power. When it didn't rain, rivers dried up, dams lost their effectiveness, and the city was forced to apply rolling blackouts to conserve the remaining energy. You can imagine Kibera, with its countless illegal electrical connections and shoddy wiring, was the first place to feel the pinch.

But most people staying in Kibera were living in rural villages one or two generations ago. They were no strangers to a life without electricity. The real struggle began with a lack of potable water. When the rivers ran dry, so did the public taps. Women who used to get water from a spigot around the corner from their home now had to carry jerry cans several kilometers on their heads. Others were forced to pay exorbitant prices to have water delivered to their house (20-30 U.S. cents for five gallons. No small fee for a person making $1 a day).

Tumaini Church's campus became a dust bowl during dry seasons in Kibera.

But again, the hardy people of Kibera could make it work. They could trudge for miles carrying water. They could bathe with less. Wash with less. The biggest implication of a lack of water, I realized, is that everything simply cost more. When it didn't rain, the price of food began to creep upwards. As rural farmers struggled to produce enough maize or beans in the dry ground, they were forced to charge more for their produce. As the price of food rose, so did the prices of other everyday items like clothing, tools, and transportation. In a community already hard-pressed economically, even small price increases could be devastating.

These three things (a lack of electricity, a shortage of water, and a rise in prices) all contributed to an overall feeling of stress and unrest in Kibera. Walking through the slum, I could see it in the faces of shopkeepers and pedestrians. Fewer smiles. Less animated conversations. Increased irritability. The stress of the drought was palpable.

One Friday night, however, the skies darkened a bit early. The wind began to blow. Everyone could smell the rain coming, but tried not to get their hopes up (it had merely drizzled the last two times this had happened). Thankfully, this was no false alarm. The dark, massive clouds broke and the rain began to fall. Heavy raindrops pounded the dirt. Pastor Fred and I slogged home through the mud, slipping all over the place and smiling the whole way.

For the first time in my life, I was actually *elated* I was being rained on. As I thought of the relief it would bring to the people of Kibera (not to mention to my own lungs and eyeballs!), I was filled with a strange sense of joy. Pastor Fred and I returned to the house exhausted and covered in mud, and I didn't mind one bit.

The following day, a new spirit was moving through the people I saw in the slum. Once again, laughter was sprinkled throughout each conversation. Children sang and played, jumping over puddles and dancing. People lined up 20 deep at their local spout to fill jerry cans that had been empty for far too long.

I would have never guessed before coming to Kibera that rain would play such a vital role in the morale of a community. When I think back to that day at the movie theater, I shake my head at how frustrated I was having to wait 10 minutes to get out to my car.

Now, I'm not going to make some sweeping statement like, "I will never take rain for granted again." Of course I will. I don't have to think about electricity or water or food when it doesn't rain for a month back home. But I do know this: the next time I'm looking out my window at a torrential downpour, I am going to think about my time in Kibera. I am going to remember those for whom precipitation is not an inconvenience, but a blessing. And I am going to pray that God would once more send dark, heavy rain clouds to that dry and dusty place.

33

Kilimanjaro

Quite a place for nature to call

A Korean man handed me his iPad. He asked me in broken English to start recording a video, then quickly joined the rest of his team behind a large white banner. They all cheered and struck a pose as one of them tried to pop the cork on a bottle of champagne. After a few moments of difficulty, the cheers stopped, but the men remained smiling in their victorious poses. Ten seconds went by. Then twenty. The man with the bottle continued to struggle.

Finally, after about a minute of awkward silence, the guy got the cork out. It made almost no noise whatsoever. The team gave a half-hearted second cheer, looked at each other with embarrassment, and stepped down to start folding up the banner. I doubt this was the moment of triumph they had envisioned when the chose to lug a bottle of champagne to the top of Mount Kilimanjaro.

I know. It's nuts. I climbed Africa's tallest mountain in

2014. In many ways, it was a grand finale for the insane amount of life change and transformation I had experienced over the ten years leading up to that moment. When I was in college in the early 2000's, I was afraid of heights, asthmatic, out of shape, and terrified of the unknown. Not a particularly strong candidate to become a mountain climber.

And yet, after climbing Volcán de Agua in Guatemala earlier that year, I had begun to dream of making it to the top of a much *higher* mountain. When the opportunity presented itself to use climbing Kilimanjaro as a fundraiser for World Next Door, I jumped at the chance.

Kilimanjaro is 19,341 feet high, the tallest free-standing mountain in the world. Because it's so wide, however, an inexperienced climber (like yours truly) can reach the top simply by walking up. There is no technical climbing involved. The only trade off is that it takes several *days* to reach the summit. In my case, the round-trip journey took six.

Joining me on my climb was Julie, one of World Next Door's summer interns, and a whole *team* of men hired to help us reach the summit (more on the absurdity of that in a moment). Neither Julie nor I had ever attempted anything like this before, so we had no idea what to expect.

The mountain, which juts out of the East African plains, has five distinct climate zones. We started our climb through a dense, green rainforest, worked our way up through heather and alpine desert, and ended the trek among arctic glaciers. As a Midwestern suburbanite from the flat-as-a-board state of Indiana, I was absolutely enthralled by the scenery. Plus, there were many species of plants and animals indigenous to Kilimanjaro that couldn't be found anywhere else in the world. It was pretty darn cool.

Most of our days were spent on *long,* six-to-eight hour hikes from one camp to the next. The Swahili words *pole pole* ("slowly slowly") became a constant refrain in the background as our guides urged us to take it slow. They knew the best way to ensure a successful summit would be if we took it nice and easy on the way up. As a result, I spent nearly the entire trek going crazy at our glacial pace.

Of course, the pace was made even slower by the fact that I had to pee *constantly*. Our guide had suggested we take Diamox, a medicine that is supposed to alleviate the symptoms of altitude sickness. The only problem was that it was also a diuretic, not a great side effect when you're supposed to be drinking three to four liters of water *every day*. Each night I had to crawl out of the tent several times to relieve myself. It was great for seeing the most incredible displays of stars I had ever witnessed. It was not so great for getting a good night's sleep.

A stream of porters carrying bags up the mountain

The main flap of my tent was broken, letting in all the chilly night air. Mostly it just hung open, held in place by a malfunctioning zipper. This kind of thing became par for the course, unfortunately, since we had inadvertently hired some pretty sketchy guides. All their gear was secondhand and it was clear they didn't take the job very seriously. One thing we found intriguing was how popular our cook was with all the other teams' porters. He was like a mini-celebrity on the mountain, greeted by many other workers as he climbed. Eventually we realized it was because he was a drug dealer, keeping all the other porters and guides well stocked with marijuana on the way up. Awesome.

About those porters. The whole system was an object lesson in how European colonialism continued to operate long after Tanzanian independence. To support the thousands of (mostly white) tourists eager to climb to Africa's tallest point, a whole *army* of indigenous guides, cooks, medics, and porters had to make the climb as well. Even though we knew our hiking companions were all relatively well paid, Julie and I were still intensely uncomfortable to see an endless stream of Tanzanian men carrying giant bags on their heads, all for the comfort of their paying guests.

This was made even more disconcerting when we realized how little the staff in charge seemed to care about the weight of our team's gear. For dinner on the third day, our "waiter" provided us with some tasty slices of watermelon. Wait, *what?!?* Watermelon? I was incredulous. They had lugged a *watermelon* up the side of a mountain for three whole days. That's got to be the least efficient calorie to weight ratio of any food they could have chosen. Apparently, they had simply decided what to bring, then calculated how many porters it would take to carry it all at their legal weight limit. Brilliant.

The whole time we climbed, we were passed by a never-ending stream of porters rushing ahead with 60 pound packs balanced on their heads to set up the next night's camp for their clients. Meanwhile, the "adventurous" paying guests had to "struggle" up the mountain carrying little more than a day pack and water bottle. At least the porters were clothed, I suppose. The first Europeans to attempt summiting Kilimanjaro had not thought to provide their gang of porters with *any* winter clothing for the glacier-capped summit (insert dramatic eye roll here).

I suppose I shouldn't complain about the inequalities. At least these porters and guides had jobs, right? They needed them, too, since so much of their ancestral land was taken away when the colonial government turned the forest around the mountain into a game reserve (oh, there go my eyes rolling again).

All that to say, once we got over the discomfort of seeing this colonialist system perpetuated, we were able to enjoy ourselves. The daily hikes were arduous, but invigorating, the scenery was spectacular, and the camaraderie we build up with our guides and the other climbers taking the same route as us was lots of fun. But nothing can compare to the sheer power of our summit morning.

Climbing Kilimanjaro was pretty cool, I guess.

To reach the summit at 19,341 feet, Julie and I had to wake up at 1am, leaving base camp in the dead of night for the seven-hour slog up to the peak. With biting winds, scant oxygen, and nothing but the light of our headlamps to guide our steps, we could do little but put one foot in front of the other and push ahead with more endurance than either of us had ever displayed before.

I was overwhelmed with emotion as I watched the sun rise over Mawenzi peak in the distance. Now that I could clearly see just how insanely high up we were, I couldn't help but become introspective. I finally understand why people talk about "mountaintop moments." My emotions were on a hair trigger, and it didn't take much for me to simply burst into tears. My biggest takeaway was simply how beautiful life is. I couldn't get over the fact that God would have allowed me to have had such an amazing experience.

I realized in that moment that my calling extended further than simply getting suburban people engaged with the poor and marginalized. It went beyond just inspiring people to do more for the kingdom of God with their time, talent, and treasure. My calling included drawing people into a life of *wonder*. I had a role to play in giving couch potatoes like my former self a glimpse at the sheer beauty and adventure of a life spent following Jesus with *everything* they had - of experiencing the joys of a life *outside* the safe suburban bubble. Life is amazing, and that's a message I needed to tell.

When we finally reached the summit, I couldn't catch my breath. My head was splitting from a terrible headache and I was nearly shaking from exhaustion. But in the midst of my discomfort, I felt a sense of accomplishment unlike anything I had ever experienced before. I had made it!

It was a profound and deeply moving moment. As I looked past glaciers to see the clouds many thousands of feet below, I was overwhelmed with feelings of gratitude, humility, and joy. Then the Diamox kicked in, so I went behind a rock and had the most scenic pee break of my entire life (super poetic, I know).

As we hurtled back down the mountain, jumping and skidding down the loose scree, I had a huge grin on my face. Every step took us deeper into the rich, thick atmosphere down below. As we spent our final night on the mountain, nothing could dampen my enthusiasm - not even the fact that rainwater poured through our cheap tents and soaked every item we owned.

I couldn't be upset. I had made it to the summit of Kilimanjaro. I had seen the sun rise from the top of Africa. I had followed Jesus into an adventure I had never imagined before. Life was very, very good.

34

Messy

Not every story has a happy ending.

When I started the book-writing process, I spent a lot of time re-reading old blog posts from my early days traveling with World Next Door. I wanted to see which stories would be worth re-telling here. Many posts brought a smile to my face or tears to my eyes as I remembered the profound tales of hope and life I had encountered. But there were a few articles that left me unsettled. I read these articles with dismay, knowing full well the neat little conclusions I had landed on were no longer so poetic.

My stories from Haiti are a good example. One happened during a visit to the impoverished village of Chambrun. My interpreter, Jean, and I were sitting on a rusty metal chair outside the home of one family's hut, chatting with them about life and watching their naked toddlers play in the dust, when something next door caught my eye.

Sitting in the shade of another hut was a young man with some sort of large metal contraption. I went over and introduced myself. His name was Bebeto (pronounced beh-bee-toe), and the device in front of him was a four-foot-long toy helicopter with *working rotors* he had constructed entirely from old soup cans and trash. Bebeto, 13 years old at the time, loved to build things and had apparently developed a real knack for circuits and electricity. Although he was quite shy and soft-spoken, the other kids looked at Bebeto with unabashed admiration in their eyes. When I asked what else he had built, the other kids got excited and started talking over each other to tell me about his other inventions.

Bebeto with his homemade toy helicopter

Although it was clear Bebeto had a lot of obstacles to overcome, including helping his mother care for the children of his sister, who died in the 2010 earthquake, I was filled with hope for the young man. Nehemiah Vision Ministries was just a 10 minute walk from his house, and I knew their school would give Bebeto a chance to get a legitimate education, even in the midst of poverty. Perhaps, I thought, he could go on to become a world-famous engineer or something. With that in mind, I wrote an article about Bebeto, thrilled at the hope and promise and potential he now had thanks to NVM and confident his life would no longer be just a statistic.

It was all good, until I bumped into Bebeto again a year later. On that trip, I was once again walking through Chambrun, when a gang of tall teenage boys passed by. One of them smiled and greeted me. I didn't even recognize him at first. Bebeto's shy boyish features had been replaced by teenage swagger. Although he still seemed like a nice kid, it seemed evident his days of "childish" tinkering were behind him.

I asked Brooke, one of the long-term nurses on staff with NVM, what had happened with him. She told me, with disappointment in her voice, that Bebeto had dropped out of school the year before, had essentially abandoned his inventions, and now spent his time wandering around with his gang of idle teenage buddies, doomed to a life of manual labor, low wages, and poverty.

I was crestfallen to hear this. Suddenly, my soaring rhetoric and boundless hope was deflated like a punctured balloon. Of course it's possible Bebeto will still beat the odds and find a way out of the cycle of poverty, but my dream of this young engineering prodigy being launched into a different kind of life had all but evaporated.

———

Something similar happened with another story I found so compelling the first time around: the story of baby Rosmelie. I first met "baby Rose" on my third visit to Haiti. It was a hot summer day, and my interpreter Denis and I decided to brave the heat to find this baby we had heard so much about. We walked down the dusty road to Chambrun, passing a few goats picking their way through the thorny scrub. The sun was high, and lizards darted across the road looking for shade. After stepping through a flimsy fence made of cacti and barbed wire, Denis and I began asking villagers where we could find baby Rosmelie and her mother. We were directed to a nearby building made of wood and mud, covered with a rusty metal roof.

Before entering the house, I took a look around. A bunch of strange objects were hanging from a tree in the front yard –

gourds strapped into miniature chairs, bottles with small bones at the bottom, tightly wrapped bundles of fabric - all voodoo religious symbols. After stepping through the open doorway, it took my eyes a second to adjust to the darkness inside. The room was empty except for a large blue barrel and a single chair. In the chair sat an 18 year old girl, holding her baby, Rosmelie.

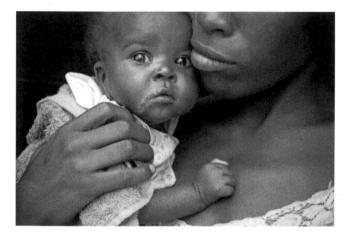

Baby Rosmelie with her mother in 2010

I walked up to them, crouched down, and spoke softly to the baby. Her alert, beautiful eyes stared up at me. As I reached down and held her hand, I could feel her tiny fingers close around mine. Normally, this would be nothing out of the ordinary. But for Rosmelie, it was nothing short of a miracle. At the time, baby Rose was an extremely malnourished six month old. She weighed 5.7 pounds. Healthy six month olds weigh more than 15. If it hadn't been for the intervention of the Nehemiah Vision Ministries medical staff, there is no question that Rosmelie would have died.

This part of the story is indisputably hopeful. NVM saved this baby's life, and as I write this she is a precocious six year old. She attends NVM's school, and has become something of a celebrity among visiting teams and volunteers. There is no doubt her life has been changed forever by that ministry.

But when I first wrote the article about Rosmelie, I was also filled with hope for her *mother*. Baby Rose's teenage mom had initially abandoned her baby. She was completely filled with despair and unwilling to take initiative to feed her child. The NVM nurses who had saved Rosmelie's life had also invested a lot of time, energy, and love into transforming the heart of her mom, and it seemed like things had begun to change. I wrote hopeful words to this effect, and ended my article about Rosmelie with visions of both the mother and the daughter's lives being redeemed.

It was all well and good, until I heard the news that Rosmelie's mom had once again abandoned Rose and left her for dead. Again, the baby was saved by NVM and this time the ministry stepped in to find a new guardian for this fragile little one. For the next couple years Rosmelie bounced around between different extended family members until finally landing in the home of an elderly aunt or grandmother or something. Hardly the poetic ending I had initially hoped for.

Again, Rosmelie is alive and healthy today, and that is entirely because of NVM. That's phenomenally hopeful. But her story became so much messier then I had initially understood. Like Bebeto's story, my tidy conclusions didn't always hold up to the uncertainties of everyday life.

———

One other example happened during my very first visit to Haiti. I had the opportunity on that trip to spend a night in NVM's children's home. As far as I understood, I was the first *blan* (white person) to stay in the village, so it was an exciting prospect. I was eager to learn what life was really like for the kids living in the home.

When I came through the gate into the small children's home property, all eight little ones were sitting on the front porch waiting for me. They were practically bouncing up and down with excitement. My stay was definitely a novelty for them. After setting up my cot in the living room, I came back outside and sat on a bench. All the kids crowded around me, laughing, giggling, and repeating Creole phrases over and over again, as if repetition would help me understand.

Eventually, the children began to settle down. A couple of them crawled up into my lap, the rest sat around me, and as the village around us became still, the kids began to sing. It was an incredibly beautiful and tender moment for me. Here I was, surrounded by children in need who were thrilled and excited simply to be close to me. It was humbling, to say the least.

When it was bedtime, I gave high fives to all the kids in their rooms and then lay down on my cot, hoping I'd be able to get some sleep in the hot, humid air. In the morning, I awoke, covered in sweat, to the sound of little girls talking quietly in the other room. I saw movement out of the corner of my eye and realized that a couple of the kids had started sneaking down the hallway to see if I was awake. I sat up and said, "Bonjou!" Within seconds, all eight children were standing around my cot, their bright eyes checking to see if I had, indeed, survived the night (I had).

The rest of the morning was spent largely the same way as the night before. We sat around, played a few games, and sang songs. When the kids realized my camera could take video, they all wanted to sing and dance to see themselves on the little screen.

Finally, it was time for me to leave, and also to receive the hardest lesson yet. I put on my backpack, walked onto the front porch, and knelt down with my arms wide. "Bye, guys! Can I have a hug?" I knew they didn't understand what I was saying, but I figured that the obvious body language of welcoming arms would give them the right idea. I was mistaken. They just stood there, looking at me with quizzical expressions on their faces.

I didn't want to be left hanging, so I gently grabbed a couple of the kids and held them close. Then, I opened my arms again and reached out to Mitanise. With a big sweet smile on her face, she walked over to me and fell backwards into my arms.

I hugged her for a few seconds, and then stood up. The rest

of the kids were still looking at me like I was playing some sort of game. The half smiles on their faces and questioning looks in their eyes revealed to me the heart-breaking truth: They didn't know how to hug. This realization shook me up. The whole drive back into town, I mulled over what I had just learned. They didn't know how to hug.

Mitanise in 2011, one of the kids in NVM's children's home

That idea was the emotional lynchpin of the article I wrote about the overnight experience. I used it as the hook to bring in hope that NVM was changing their lives. There is only one problem with this as I look back on what I wrote. I'm not even sure it's true.

The more I've traveled and engaged with new cultures and ministries, the more I've realized how little I genuinely understand about what I'm seeing in front of me. I have been guilty, on more than one occasion, of coming to completely inaccurate conclusions based on my cultural presuppositions. Looking back at this early article with more experienced eyes, I can see all sorts of elements I didn't factor in before making my sweeping conclusion - so many questions I never thought to ask.

Is hugging a significant part of Haitian culture? Do fathers in Chambrun generally hug their children? Do men hug at all? Were there different nonverbal cues I could have been giving? Were these kids allowed to hug strangers? Were they just being shy? For me to assume based on the minuscule amount of information I actually had about the situation - that these kids had never been taught how to hug - was quite a leap.

—

What I've begun to realize as I look back at the hundreds of articles I've written over the last six years is that life is messy. As much as I want to wrap everything up in a tidy little box, not every story has a happy ending. Not everything I see can be summed up in a single idea. In a world full of sinful, broken people, there will be some defeats among our victories.

But in the midst of this sobering reality check, something surprising has been happening in my heart. I've actually become even *more* hopeful than I was before. Looking at the broad sweep of stories I've told for the past half-decade, I can see a clear pattern emerging. God is working in the world.

For every disappointing story like Bebeto's, there are five stories like little Peter's in Ukraine, whose brilliant adoption far outshone the glimmer of hope I had described in my first article about him. For every bittersweet tale like baby Rosmelie and her mother, there are ten overwhelmingly beautiful stories in which an entire *family* is redeemed. Over and over, light beats back the darkness, lives are transformed, and the kingdom of God expands into our broken world.

That's why I am not discouraged as I look back to see some messiness in the articles I've written. It's a reminder that the world I encountered in my travels was *real*. Yes, pursuing God's heart for humanity's redemption is a bumpy, uncertain path, but the ministries I met are walking along it faithfully. The Holy Spirit is guiding their steps. When all is said and done, hope *will* prevail.

35

Raised Arms

Plaques are overrated anyway.

In the fall of 2011, I did something a bit crazy. I took a group of young businessmen and the CEO of an international company into Kibera Slum. These men and I had been part of a discipleship group together for a couple of years. This mostly consisted of bi-monthly conference calls in which we discussed matters of life and faith. However, on this particular year, when our group's leader, Jeff, asked if anyone had any unique ideas for our annual team retreat, I half-jokingly said, "Let's go to Kenya!"

Only a couple guys in the group had ever been to the developing world before, and *none* had been to Africa, so I didn't expect much to come of the suggestion. Imagine my surprise, then, when the response was completely positive! The team actually wanted to go. So we started the prep work for the trip through the summer, and in October we got on a plane bound for Nairobi.

As we traveled around the city and engaged with partner

ministries like Tumaini Church and Beacon of Hope, I worked hard to break free from the standard "missions trip" model. By that point in my life, I had seen so many short term trips that did more harm than good. I had no interest in leaving behind us a wake of frustration and unfulfilled promises when our trip was through.[10]

The team with Pastor Fred and his family at his home in Kibera

Instead of coming to Kenya with an agenda like constructing a building or leading a vacation Bible school, we focused primarily on simply *learning* from local leaders. Our time with Pastor Fred in Kibera was especially fruitful. Listening to his perspective on leadership, spiritual development, and faith was a tremendous eye-opener for our whole team. Seeing the work of Tumaini Church in the slum was compelling and exciting for all of us. The ministry wasn't flashy, but it was clearly having a deep impact on its community.

---

[10] Again, to get a much deeper understanding of what I'm describing here, pick up *When Helping Hurts* by Brian Fikkert and Steve Corbett. The book is incredibly useful!

Towards the end of our time in Kibera, the guys on my team began to feel led by God to make a financial gift to Tumaini. I was thrilled at their willingness, but laid out a few ground rules before we made any promises.

First, the money would have to be as anonymous as possible. Obviously, Pastor Fred would know it was from us, but I had zero desire to see our names on a plaque somewhere. Second, the funds would be for a project of Tumaini's choosing. We wouldn't tell them what to do with it. They would tell us what *they* dreamed of accomplishing. Finally, the money would need to be completely undesignated. In other words, once it was in the hands of Pastor Fred and his team, there would be no strings attached. We would have to trust the team at Tumaini to handle the funds with integrity.

With all of those ground rules in place, the guys still felt compelled to give, so we pulled Pastor Fred aside and sat down for a chat. At one point in the conversation, I asked Fred, "If money was not an obstacle, what would you do next to grow the ministry of Tumaini Church?"

He didn't skip a beat in responding. "We'd build new classrooms for our students, construct a bigger sanctuary for our community, and dig new pit latrines for better sanitation."

"And how much would all that cost?" I asked.

He thought for a moment and said, "Probably about $10,000."

The guys all looked at each other, smiled, and said, "Done. We will find that money for you. Go make it happen!" Pastor Fred was understandably elated.

Before we closed the meeting, one of young businessmen asked Fred if we could pray for him. Fred agreed. Just before we started praying, however, one of the other guys, named Dave, said, "Um, this might be a bit weird, but would it be OK if we held your arms up in the air while we prayed?"

He quickly explained the reference. In Exodus 17, the Israelites were fighting the Amalekites. Whenever Moses held his staff up in the air, the Israelites would be winning the battle. When he let his arms drop, they'd start to lose.

Eventually Moses' arms grew tired, so Aaron and Hur came alongside and held his hands up for him. This was a perfect image, Dave explained, of how we saw our role in Kibera. Pastor Fred was Moses, God's instrument in the battle. We were simply coming alongside to help Fred accomplish the purpose God had set out for him.

As we prayed blessings and encouragements over Fred that afternoon, we held his arms in the air. It was clear the moment was an emotional one for him. Tears streamed down his face as he felt the love and support of the global Church, along with the dignity and trust of men who wanted to see *him* succeed in his God-given mission.

When we were done praying, Fred looked up and said, "Right after this meeting I was going to lead a Bible study in the room next door. The passage I had prepared to teach was Exodus 17."

We were all overjoyed at how the Spirit had orchestrated the moment. Our team came back to the US dedicated to raising the $10,000 we'd promised. By the middle of the following month, construction had already begun on the new buildings on Tumaini's campus. However, the story was not over yet. Little did any of us know there was an even more providential moment ahead.

In July of 2012, eight months after Tumaini completed their new construction, I had the chance to once more travel to Nairobi and spend time with Pastor Fred. Unfortunately, he had some bad news to share. It seemed the Kenyan government had decided to bulldoze a large swath of Kibera to make way for a highway bypass road. The construction workers set up markers to show where they'd be plowing, and later that year made good on their promise.

The tragic reality of this demolition was that it ran right through Tumaini's campus. Fully half of their existing property, including most of their classroom buildings, had to go. Under normal circumstances, this would have crippled the school. With no buildings for the students to study in, they'd have no way to keep their doors open. It would have essentially *ended* their ministry.

Thankfully, these weren't normal circumstances. God had been orchestrating something quite remarkable. As it turned out, the school did *not* have to close up shop. Why? Because they now had a new, larger sanctuary and a whole new row of sturdy classrooms for the students to use. The classrooms had been build literally *feet* away from where the bulldozers ran. Thanks to the Holy Spirit's promptings, God had used the young businessmen I had brought to Kenya to accomplish his purposes. The construction project had been able to move forward years ahead of schedule. It was just in time, it turned out, to keep the school operational in the midst of this unforeseen crisis.

I get so fired up when I think about this story. It's such a simple, but beautiful depiction of the global Church partnering together. The American team learned at the feet of leaders like Pastor Fred, coming home with a new perspective on the world, a deeper understanding of faith, and greater potential for leadership. The Kenyan leaders we partnered with got an influx of fresh encouragement, an expansion of their network of prayer support, and new financial resources with which to operate their ministry. In this moment, the American and Kenyan churches did more together than we could have ever done apart.

I still have a lot of reservations when I think about how easy it is for short term trips to do more harm than good. But after experiences like this, I have hope that one day we'll learn how to partner together to see God's kingdom spread more powerfully than it ever has before.

36

Uncharted Lands

Not all ravines have an other side.

Sometimes I like to describe my faith journey as exploring an uncharted land. I wander through the wilderness, guided by God's voice beckoning me to take step after step into the unknown. Every now and then, I come across a chasm blocking my way - some obstacle to faith that needs to be crossed before I can continue on my trek.

In elementary school, it was a simple one. "Does God even exist?" Like a steep ravine opening in the ground ahead of me, the question forced me to find an answer before I could move on. Thankfully, I found a bridge - the faith of my parents, grandparents, and community. I could see evidence of God's existence in the way they lived their lives, and it gave me the confidence to cross to the other side. I kept walking.

In high school and college, the question became, "Am I willing to surrender my *life* to Jesus?" All of my own hopes and dreams and plans were a new kind of obstacle blocking my way. Again, I found a way across the gap - a tall tree with vines

I could swing on. I tasted the fruit and joy and adventure that would come from a life fully dedicated to the kingdom and landed on the opposite side. I continued on my journey.

After college, I wondered, "Is God trustworthy?" To cross *that* crevasse, I had to run full steam ahead and leap into the unknown. Scared to death at first, I traveled the world and lived in dangerous places and watched as God came through for me time and time again. Arms flailing and heart pumping, I made it in one piece to the other side and my road continued on.

But in the spring of 2009, I encountered a chasm so wide I have yet to find a way across. It happened when I met Nastya, a little girl being cared for by Mission to Ukraine in the city of Zhytomyr. Nastya was severely disabled. Confined to a wheelchair and unable to move, she had very few means of communication with those around her. One thing she *could* do, though, was smile. And boy, did she ever smile. Sitting in class with Nastya, I'd make a face or do something goofy and watch as she lit up with the most brilliant expression of joy I've ever seen. It absolutely broke my heart.

I was obviously thrilled to see her so joyful, and I couldn't have been happier that Mission to Ukraine was there to love her so well, but I simply couldn't stop asking God, "Why?"

Why is Nastya disabled? *Why* was she born with this degenerative condition? How could this possibly be a part of God's plan?

I understood, to some extent, how children suffering from poverty or hunger were in that place because of the sinfulness of man. Greed, corruption, and pride have taken their toll on the last and least of the world. But how could this beautiful girl, who will most likely die long before her time, be in such a horrible place?

I searched the edges of this chasm, longing for some way across. I found no bridge. No rope. No jetpack. All I had was the assurance from scripture that God is good and his heart breaks even more than mine at the darkness of this shattered world.

And that's where I am today. Continuing my exploration of the uncharted lands before me. Sometimes I return to the chasm, wondering if I'll ever find a way across. But the more I visit the edge of this cliff, the more I am convinced that I may never have an answer on this side of eternity.

As I walk, I clutch the image of Nastya's smile close to my heart and long for the day when God's kingdom will come in all its fullness. When there will be no more tears. When there will be no more pain. And when there will be no more chasms to cross.

Acknowledgments

I've got to come clean real quick. I have no idea how to write a book. I mean, I *did* just write one, but I still don't know what I'm doing. If it wasn't for the help of many tremendous people, this book would have never gotten off the ground.

Thanks, first of all, to my parents, who graciously read every chapter the moment I finished each rough draft. Your encouragement helped me to keep at it, especially when I was walking around telling everyone, "Don't *ever* let me write a book again!" Plus, mom? You're a killer copy editor. Typos tell horror stories about you to scare their children into behaving.

Thanks to Curtis for all your feedback about cover design, interior layout, etc. The fact that we painstakingly made the horizontal lines match the width of the chapter numbers made all the difference in the world. Thanks also to Tara for convincing me to adopt modern writing standards like the Oxford comma, the single space after a period, and not using too many freaking ellipses…

Thanks, of course, to Brad, Sharon, Jess, Kaiti, and Ron, who read the rough draft of the book and provided such amazingly valuable feedback.

Zooming out just a bit, I want to include a *huge* thank-you to the hundreds of donors, readers, prayer-team members, summer interns, year-long fellows, and advisors who made World Next Door possible in the first place. It's been a wild ride. And even though I still blame each of you for making me eat goat brains, I wouldn't trade the last six years for anything.

Words can't even come close to capturing the gratitude I feel for all the wonderful hosts, partners, leaders, teachers, and friends I have met around the world. You've opened your homes, you've taught me so much, and you have demonstrated the love of Christ in the way you live your lives. Now that I know you, I will never be the same.

Finally, I want to thank my savior, Jesus, for believing in me despite my many shortcomings. I am humbled every day that you want to use me for your kingdom purposes. I still sometimes wish you'd clue me in on what lies ahead, but you've never let me down before. I can't imagine you'd start now. I am humbled by your grace and astounded by your sacrifice. May your kingdom come and will be done on earth as it is in heaven!

TRAVEL CALENDAR

2009

Kenya – Tumaini Church
Ukraine – Mission to Ukraine
Indianapolis – Shepherd Community Center
Haiti – Nehemiah Vision Ministries
Panama – Dead Wheat International Foundation

2010

Haiti – Nehemiah Vision Ministries
New York City – The Relief Bus
Ukraine – Mission to Ukraine
India – Truthseekers International
Cambodia – The Center for Global Impact, Rapha House

2011

Haiti – Nehemiah Vision Ministries
Holy Land – Musalaha
Kenya – Tumaini Church

2012

Penelakut Island – Reclaiming Original
Outdoor Activities and Skills
South Africa – Loving South Africa
Ukraine – Mission to Ukraine

2013

Cambodia – The Center for Global Impact
Rwanda/South Sudan – African Leadership
and Reconciliation Ministries
Guatemala – Saber y Gracia
Haiti – Nehemiah Vision Ministries

2014

Guatemala – Saber y Gracia
Kenya – Tumaini Church
Ukraine – Mission to Ukraine

PARTNER MINISTRIES

In order of appearance

Mission to Ukraine
Zhytomyr, Ukraine
missiontoukraine.org

Tumaini Church
Nairobi, Kenya

Nehemiah Vision Ministries
Chambrun, Haiti
nvm.org

African Leadership and Reconciliation Ministries (ALARM)
Juba, South Sudan
alarm-inc.org

Nairobi Chapel
Nairobi, Kenya
nairobichapel.org

Truthseekers International
New Delhi, India
truthseekersinternational.org

Rapha House
Phnom Penh, Cambodia
raphahouse.org

New York City Relief
Elizabeth, New Jersey
reliefbus.org

Musalaha
Jerusalem, Israel
musalaha.org

Sewa Ashram (Delhi House Society)
New Delhi, India
delhihouse.org

Saber y Gracia (Wisdom and Grace)
Santo Tomás Milpas Altas, Guatemala
wisdomandgrace.org

The Center for Global Impact
Phnom Penh, Cambodia
centerforglobalimpact.org

Reclaiming Original Outdoor Technology and Skills (ROOTS)
Penelakut Island, British Columbia
naim.ca

ABOUT THE AUTHOR

Barry Rodriguez is a pastor at Grace Church in Noblesville, Indiana and the founder of World Next Door, Inc. He has a Biblical Studies degree from Moody Bible Institute and has visited 26 different countries so far.

A self-proclaimed dilettante, Barry's interests include backpacking, travel, anthropology, photography, science fiction, world history, graphic design, astrophysics, and hand-stitching leather goods. He lives in Indianapolis.

To watch some of Barry's sermons, visit gracechurch.us/sermons

To take a look at Barry's travel photography, visit barryrodphotography.com

To get in touch with Barry, drop him a line at barry.d.rodriguez@gmail.com

20836551R00133

Made in the USA
San Bernardino, CA
26 April 2015